The
Graphic Design
Exercise Book

A RotoVision Book

Published and distributed by RotoVision SA
Route Suisse 9
CH-1295 Mies
Switzerland

RotoVision SA
Sales and Editorial Office
Sheridan House, 114 Western Road
Hove BN3 1DD, UK

Tel: +44 (0)1273 72 72 68
Fax: +44 (0)1273 72 72 69
www.rotovision.com

While every effort has been made to contact
owners of copyright material produced in this book,
we have not always been successful. In the event
of a copyright query, please contact the Publisher.

10 9 8 7 6 5 4 3 2 1

ISBN: 978-2-88893-050-1

Art Director: Tony Seddon
Design: Morris & Winrow
Typeface: Glypha LT and Interstate
Reprographics in Singapore by ProVision Pte.
Tel: +65 6334 7720
Fax: +65 6334 7721

Printed in China by 1010 Printing International Ltd.

The
Graphic Design Exercise Book

Creative Briefs to Enhance Your Skills and Develop Your Portfolio

Carolyn Knight and Jessica Glaser

RotoVision

Contents

in each section ...

briefs are aimed at different levels of experience and
competency. Each brief is marked with a difficulty
rating as follows:

●○○   Introductory

●●○   Intermediate

●●●   Advanced

Introduction

Graphic designers love the excitement of an inspiring and creative challenge, with the quest to expand knowledge and skills often at the forefront of their minds. Many varied disciplines come together to give this unique profession great breadth, and it can be hard to gain experience in all areas. A designer's portfolio should be an ever-evolving demonstration of ability and enthusiasm, but the demands of work can make this difficult. Smaller design studios and agencies are often restricted by the type of work their clients require—it can be very stimulating to take up the challenge of "having a go" at something different. This book provides a wide spectrum of briefs and working methodologies with a view to giving designers the opportunity to try new disciplines or expand existing ones, to fire their creativity, and to acquire new professional skills. It is also a tool for recent graduates wishing to enhance and expand their portfolios in order to find a place within the world of graphic design.

The Graphic Design Exercise Book has five sections, each focusing on a specific graphic design genre: packaging, visual identity and branding, page layout, design for music, and design for screen. As visual identity and branding have a strong impact on all other graphic design disciplines, this is the largest section. Each section includes a glossary, a list of the equipment typically required, and a reading list. Most aspects of graphic design require some specialist knowledge, particularly in relation to the use of software, materials, and formats. They also tend to possess unique vocabularies that can be intimidating and somewhat daunting to those not "in the know." The glossaries are intended to help readers feel more comfortable with the kind of language used in the methodologies and the reading lists provide a helpful starting point for subject-specific research.

The stand-alone projects in each section allow readers to select a brief that is suited to their own level of interest, experience, and available time. They are presented in order of complexity so that designers tackling an unfamiliar discipline can try their hand at each brief in order to gradually build up competency and confidence in their new skills. In addition to a complete brief, each project offers advice on working methodologies from the research stage, through exploration and developing thumbnails, to design development and completion. Quotes from a range of industry experts offer valuable advice drawn from real-world experience.

For each project, designs from international designers are showcased. Use this reference material for research into different aspects of a design, including color reference, use of language, subject matter, typographic relationships, format, materials, and style of art direction. Don't plagiarize the work, but do use it for inspiration. It is impossible to seek out too much visual inspiration—the reference sections of this book are as packed and stimulating as possible, but you should use them only as the starting point for your own research.

A mixture of hand-generated roughs and computer visuals shows a variety of sample responses to each brief. All these elements are annotated with professional feedback. Judging the success of a design solution can be a challenge. Ask for feedback on your own work, read back through the methodology section of the brief, and read through the comments that accompany the sample solutions for each brief. However innovative and original a design may be, it is still important that it adheres to a number of systems and conventions: cross-referencing comments on student solutions could help you pick up and remedy weaknesses in your own design.

A computer is listed in many of the equipment lists, and this includes appropriate professional design software. We have suggested, for all the projects in this book, that your initial exploration and thumbnails should be hand-generated in order to maximize your creative potential rather than be restricted to working within the limitations of your technical know-how. However, in order to make the most of the opportunities presented, it is advisable to translate hand-generated roughs onto a computer.

The Completion advice for most of the briefs refers to both print and online portfolios. You may wish to produce your own website to display your designs, or you may prefer to use one of the many commercial options available. These can be found simply by searching for "online portfolios" via any search engine.

Section 01
Packaging

Packaging design, the area of graphic design the public has most contact with, is also one of the most complex as it involves both 2D and 3D design: surface graphics and construction. These challenging and thought-provoking briefs require a considerable amount of research effort.

Many consumers feel that packaging is simply waste. The media makes the most of statistics regarding the environmental impact of post-consumer waste, bombarding the public with details of materials that end up in landfill sites. However, packaging does perform an often unrecognized role. In order to function and profit in a global economy, producers are required to store, distribute, and market their products, and this would not be possible without packaging. Effective packaging significantly reduces pre-consumer food waste. Ian Williamson, head of retail at Tetra Pak, reinforces this point. "Packaging helps reduce the amount of carbon emission in the supply chain by extending the shelf life of foodstuffs. Well-packaged foods don't go off as quickly, which means smaller quantities are wasted and less goes to landfill to create methane."

Environmental considerations are important for the packaging designer, but communication between producer and consumer is a vital factor that must not be overlooked. On store shelves packaging is the main selling tool for products; shoppers may make a purchase as a result of advertising, but mostly they will buy a product in response to the visual language and information on the pack. Packaging provides the designer with a unique challenge not only to protect and preserve, but also to present quality design that functions in both 2D and 3D contexts.

01 Client: Okanagan Spring Brewery
Design: Subplot Design

02 Client: NapaStyle
Design: Design by Principle

Amy-Claire Morgan
Customer Marketing Director

In contrast to many other graphic design disciplines, packaging design can make use of a multitude of print and production techniques and a great variety of materials. Explore the practicalities and implications of using different materials. It is essential that any materials you choose function appropriately—for example, that they keep moisture off a dried product, or prevent a fragile product being damaged. However, you must also keep in mind that certain substrates are linked with certain values: tea packaged in a card box or paper bag can convey a thrifty approach for an everyday tea, whereas metal containers are likely to suggest a more luxurious product of premium quality. Similarly, print techniques can play a major role in communicating brand value and creating customer appeal. For example, embossing and foil blocking can position the product in the "traditional" market, whereas varnish and laminate can make a product seem more stylish and modern.

Surface graphics also play an important role, and must function equally well on every side of a package. As Matthew Clark of Subplot Design says, "The package is a whole, not just the sum of its parts. Every panel should communicate the brand proposition and the overall design platform to the same extent. When I am dealing with beverages, which often demand massive amounts of additional copy or nutrition facts panels, I make sure I spend just as much time designing, perfecting, kerning, and finessing the back panels as I do the front. The result is a whole package, not one with a great front and throwaway sides and back."

03 Project: Eco packaging
Design: Amy Morgan

04 Client: Calistoga Bakery Café
Design: Vrontikis Design Office

01 Project: Cosmetics
packaging
Design: Lotte Hammergren
Andresen

01

With the advent of highly advanced computer programs and large-scale, high-quality monitors, there is a temptation to simply assess a packaging design on-screen. Inevitably, in these circumstances, focus is mainly on a front face, as the other sides are quite often only seen upside down. It is important to consider all sides individually and collectively—success in a 2D rendering does not always translate to success in the 3D realm.

The visual identity and brand values expressed through packaging design play a vital role in successful communication with an audience. Choices of typeface, color, composition, and imagery all influence the context and target market in which a product will be placed. Comparatively subtle changes can achieve significant shifts in positioning and appeal. For example, a change in hue from bright blue to a softer tertiary blue can move a product from a youth market to a more sophisticated, mature audience.

Generally, the use of composition and scale can result in clear demarcations between upmarket, expensive products and cheaper, less aspirational alternatives. Packaging for the latter frequently involves busy layouts that include a mix of alignments and similarities of scale; designs for upmarket products tend to adopt a minimalist approach, with dramatic areas of space and dynamic contrasts of scale.

Packaging is particularly subject to the influence of visual cues established by key brands; certain colors, typefaces, images, and other graphic elements have become synonymous with particular products and brands, and designers choosing to ignore these cues run the risk of losing an audience. However, the packaging designer's dilemma is even more complex. As Matthew Clark says, "I believe every package should balance category cues (which are good) with category clichés (which are very, very bad). On the one hand, the temptation for many young designers (and naive clients) is to simply mirror a category look, particularly when introducing a new product. The problem here is that the solution does not break through the clutter and clichés that develop in a given category. Why do all snowboards have images of cool guys doing cool tricks? Why does every high-end perfume have the same minimalist aesthetic? One of the designer's roles is to help the client stand out in a cluttered marketplace, and playing to clichés doesn't do this. However, the opposite temptation—ignoring category cues—is not helpful either. Cues are what help the consumer understand that one bottle is juice and another is milk. It does nobody any good to defy the category norms and design a beer bottle that the consumer mistakes for motor oil!"

02 Client: Calistoga Bakery Café
Design: Vrontikis Design Office

02

ALWAYS APRICOT

Calistoga

RASPBERRY TART

Diamond Creek
Raspberry Jam

NET WT 10 OZ (280g)

Calistoga

the simple life.™

Glossary

alignment the arrangement of image and text in a design, typically from a left, right, central, top, or bottom axis

annotation comment on a design rough or concept that gives information additional to what can be shown in the rough

bleed when a page or design extends to and off the edge of the paper or trimmed edge of a pack, it is called a "bleed"

body copy/body type the main text excluding headlines and subheads; for the purpose of visuals this can be nonsensical

brand identity the visual image the public has of a product

brand value the impression that the public has of a product

cliché a stereotypical design choice that lacks "freshness"

elements of design the building blocks of design: color, shape, size, space, line, value, and texture

embossing a print technique that raises the surface of the substrate

foil blocking an inkless print technique that stamps a design by using a colored foil and pressure from a heated die or block

four-color process/full-color process a printing process that reproduces colors by combining cyan, magenta, yellow, and black

genre an artistic type or style, an area of expertise

hierarchy (visual) the arrangement of elements to guide viewers through them in a specific order

hue color or gradation of color, e.g. red, blue-green, dusty pink

kerning the space between individual letterforms

leading the space between lines of type

logo/logotype distinctive visual character created by the design of the letters that constitute a product name; a namestyle

maquette 3D model, often in miniature

marker paper specialist flimsy paper with a coating that prevents marker pens from bleeding through

namestyle see logo/logotype

sans serif a style of typeface without serifs, i.e., without ornamental strokes on the ends of characters. Common sans serif typefaces include Arial, Helvetica, AvantGarde, and Verdana

strapline a line of text that sums up the unique selling point(s) of a product

substrate the material that a pack is made of

symbol a distinctive image or mark that represents a product; generally works with a namestyle

system (design system) a number of things organized in relation to each other to form a considered whole

thumbnails comparatively small rough visuals that incorporate sufficient detail and accuracy to be of value for decision-making

tracking the letterspacing applied across a line of text

visual code/visual cue visual element or group of elements that have a definite connotation due to frequency of use in similar situations

visual language a meaningful language created by visual elements other than words

Reading list

1000 Bags, Tags & Labels:
Provocative Packaging for
All Products
Cheryl Dangel Cullen

1000 Package Designs:
A Complete Compilation
of Creative Containers
Grip Design

The Designer's Packaging Bible:
Creative Solutions for
Outstanding Design
Luke Herriott

Graphis Packaging Design 9
Martin Pederson

The Little Book of Big
Packaging Ideas
Catharine Fishel and Stacey King Gordon

Packaging 01: An Essential Primer
for Today's Competitive Market
Capsule

The Packaging and Design
Templates Sourcebook
Luke Herriott

Structural Package Designs
Haresh Pathak

Structural Packaging: Workbook
Josep M. Garrofe

What Is Packaging Design?
Giles Calver

Equipment

- Scalpel
- Marker paper
- Pencils
- Markers/colored pencils
- Steel ruler
- Set square
- Typeface reference
- Cutting mat
- Double-sided tape
- Low-tack adhesive tape
- Adhesive tape
- Matte finish invisible adhesive tape
- Spray adhesive
- Lightweight card
- Professional color matching reference
- Computer/software

Brief 01

Eco-friendly laundry packaging

The brief

Design packaging for new eco-friendly laundry product ecocleen, using the logo supplied

PMS 284   PMS 375

The brief explained

Target market

ecocleen is not targeted at a specific age group; it should appeal to all consumers of laundry products who have an environmental awareness and conscience and who choose to prioritize the purchase of "green" items. Buying ecocleen should make the consumer feel good about being responsible and caring for the planet.

Requirements

Design one pack for laundry product ecocleen. You may select the carton size and choose to package either washing powder or washing tablets. Analyze the visual elements used within the product namestyle provided and develop surface graphics for the front, top, and sides of this packaging based on maximizing their scope.

Use this logo in your designs for the ecocleen packaging brief.

Methodology

Research

Look at existing laundry product packaging, especially eco products. Take note of a variety of packages related to environmentally friendly or natural goods; while many may not have a close association with washing or cleaning, their package designs are likely to reflect "eco" connections. The namestyle provided defines the two colors of the pack, but it is valuable to appreciate how space and pattern are used within the designs of the packs for similar products. Note how busy or calm the designs are; look at the content of supporting information and how it is presented. The namestyle is given as PMS 284 blue and PMS 375 green on white, but is it appropriate to have a white background, or should one of the colors become the background hue with part of the namestyle reversed through?

The pack has six sides, all of which must be designed. The sixth side—the base—contains manufacturer's details, usage information, and any legally required details. All of these elements must be styled in a manner that is sympathetic to the overall visual concept. Observe how existing boxes deal with ordering information on each face and how each side relates to the others hierarchically. Most boxes have a front that displays type and image in an eye-catching manner for strong impact on the supermarket shelves. The other sides support the front, possibly containing more text or having less dominant content. Consider whether the pack is to be landscape or portrait when displayed, think about the opening and closing mechanisms and incorporate them into the design. Look for design techniques that allow the visual elements to run over more than one side, and also study how the folds and corners of the packs are treated.

Exploration and thumbnails

Analyze every detail of the given namestyle as all aspects of the design must stem from the style of the letterforms, the manner in which they come together, and the formation of any illustrative elements. Additional elements can be introduced, but they should associate with and complement the character of the product logo rather than dominate the design. Find a couple of markers and/or crayons that are close to the two colors of the namestyle and sketch alternative designs for the pack on marker paper. This enables a much freer approach, as it is considerably easier to move from one concept to an entirely different idea on paper than it is on computer.

Design development

It is very important to spend time exploring a number of ideas rather than settling for the most obvious solution and simply making minor alterations and subtle tweaks to that. Reference the design principles of existing packs; be inspired by ideas from a number of examples. Trace visuals from one page to another with the marker paper, replicating sections you want to keep and redrawing areas that need amending. At any point it may be appropriate to create a concept, or part of a concept, on the computer, moving between pen and paper and computer until you find a successful solution.

The unique characteristic of packaging design is that it involves a 3D item that will have one or more sides hidden at any one time. Visuals can be created for one side at a time, but it is more helpful if, right from the beginning, you embrace all of the "exposed" sides and show how they relate to each other.

In this brief the pack is the standard pack used to contain laundry tablets or powder. Buy an existing pack fairly early on in your design process and use this as a dummy, applying rough visuals to all sides so that you can assess and address their relationship. Deconstruct the pack carefully to become familiar with its overall structure. This will help you construct smaller versions—maquettes—which, in turn, will help you make informed judgments concerning design alternatives. There is no replacement for handling a 3D mock-up of a package, even if it is only made from paper. The process gives a real sense of how the package will finally appear at point of sale, and how it will be used in the home. Until a design is put together in the form of a box, it is impossible to be aware of both the cohesion and coherence of all the sides. It is particularly important to take note of angles within a design; they may appear visually comfortable "in the flat," but run in unexpected directions and fight with each other in 3D form.

To be successful a package must look good on its own, as it will appear in the home, and also in groups, sitting side by side and next to competitor brands on the store shelves. Remember to stand back and assess your designs frequently. It can also be helpful to ask other people what they think of your design.

The images here show examples of packaging design that have an obvious regard for the environment and contain products that are natural in origin or makeup. Although these designs are not for laundry brands, the lessons to be learned from them are easily transferable.

01/02 Natural Planet
Design: Stormhouse Partners

02

01

03

03 Client: RAWphoriaLIVE
Design: Sayles Graphic Design

04 Client: SMS
Design: Studio International

05 Client: Paddywax
Design: Design by Principle

Completion

Make up your solutions for the ecocleen pack and photograph them carefully from a number of angles. You can also show images of the pack designs in context, next to competitors on the store shelves. Be sure to ask permission from the store manager before photographing your pack in context. Display your printouts on a neutral background. Online presentation is also a very practical way to display your design solutions. You can upload your work, as a PDF or as separate images, to your own site or to commercial portfolio sites.

Ecover is a market leader and a pioneering force in environmentally friendly laundry products. When designing packaging for a specific sector, it is always advisable to observe such market leaders; decide whether it is necessary to emulate some of the visual codes or whether you can flout them and forge a new approach.

Client: Ecover (in-house)
Design: Ecover

ECOLOGICAL
WASHING LIQUID
FOR FINE FABRICS
AND WOOL
WOOLMARK ®

ECOVER®
DELICATE

for people who care

ECOLOGICAL
WASHING-UP LIQUID
WITH LEMON AND ALOE VERA

ECOVER®

NATURALLY MILD ON YOUR HANDS

for people who care

Solutions

Project: Eco-friendly laundry packaging
Design: Bright Pink

As ecocleen, the namestyle for this brief, is provided, the student work shown uses the namestyle Green Wash to give guidance for appropriate ways of working without preempting solutions.

There are two concepts, based predominantly on the decorative rows of small leaves: the first, which focuses on the linear pattern they create, is set on a white background; the second uses the leaves to work with the transition from a blue to a white background. The larger leaves are used as a space in which to set the necessary product information.

The design with the wide turquoise band would run this element around the pack, probably with a large namestyle reversed through on the front. The color in the background enables part of the logo to be white through, and the leaves are used at contrasting scales. Generally speaking, contrast of scale and composition are essential ingredients of design.

Project: Eco-friendly laundry packaging
Design: Bright Pink

This design, with the namestyle reversed through turquoise at the top and blue at the bottom, splits the background colors following the division of the namestyle, bringing in the bands of color over the top and bottom rather than from the sides. A horizontal row of tiny leaves is used to disguise some of the problems with the descender of the "g" and the ascender of the "h;" however, two further computer-generated thumbnails look at resolving this detailing in different configurations. Alternating between hand-generated visuals and more resolved work on the computer is ideal for allowing freedom of creativity alongside limitations imposed by production methods.

"The words 'green' and 'wash' are staggered and sit on two different baselines, and the text and tinted text boxes reflect this relationship. It is important that the subtleties in the configuration and style of a logo are recognized and used to influence and inspire other relationships and design treatments in a solution."

Carolyn Knight and Jessica Glaser, Bright Pink

Project: Eco-friendly laundry packaging
Design: Bright Pink

In this maquette the designer is expanding the involvement of both the signature colors and the two leaves that sit behind the "ee" in green. The namestyle is in blue and turquoise on white, but on this pack the strong blue is used as a background color on some of the sides, with the "g" of the logo reversed through in white or turquoise. This type of role reversal in colors is a powerful tool that enables you to create more dynamic contrasts of scale and spatial distribution as it helps you avoid large empty white areas. It is worth considering running designs over the edges of packs, as in this concept, as this forces you to handle all sides at once and can lead to a more coherent whole. The leaves are introduced, in a number of sizes, both as a decorative border along the perimeter of the blue background and as pale shapes to contain subsidiary text.

The white pack with scattered leaves uses the "leaf pair" to create a wallpaper effect on the front face of the pack; leaves are used as part of the namestyle to suggest the natural ingredients in the washing powder. By angling and repeating them as though they are blowing across the pack, the designers have introduced the idea of fresh air and breezes—the natural way to dry clothes. The solid blue, which is used as a background to information that has to be included on the other sides, acts as a contrast to the lighter and visually busier front.

"I believe that most designers actually forget that a package is a 3D object. Print designers are used to the ideas of pagination, sequence, and a front and back. While there is certainly a principal display panel to any given package, the consumer is free to interact with the object as a whole."

Matthew Clark, Subplot Design

Project: Eco-friendly laundry packaging
Design: Bright Pink

In the thumbnail that depicts two large leaves on a blue background, the "leaf pair" plays the dominant role in defining the pack. It is likely that consumers familiar with the product would recognize the simple shapes and colors of the leaves over and above the namestyle. A good logo always provides a number of design elements that can be used with varying degrees of prominence and your thumbnails should exploit as many variations as possible. Note that not all sides have blue backgrounds—this could make the pack rather monotonous. The computer-generated versions substitute two leaf prints for the "leaf pair" and show compositional and proportional alternatives.

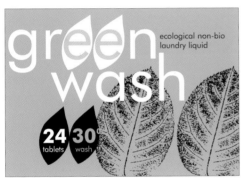

Brief 02

Tea packaging

The brief
Design a range of tea packaging

The brief explained
Target market
The target market is the health-conscious, predominantly female consumer, aged 25+, who usually drinks tea and fruit or herbal infusions. This range should also entice new consumers who are looking for a healthy alternative to coffee and other hot beverages. This product should help the consumer feel good about making an effort to maintain a healthy lifestyle and should also appeal to individuals who prioritize spending to ensure personal fitness and well-being.

Requirements
Design the structural packaging and surface graphics for a new range of tea bags. The range includes three types of tea and each pack contains 20 tea bags. Choose varieties or names for the new range, for example, Morning Tea, Afternoon Tea, and Evening Tea. Develop a descriptive strapline for each variety to explain the character, quality, flavor, and properties of each. Surface graphics must include the product name, strapline, quantities, ingredients, and any other statutory requirements (check existing boxes of tea for this information), as well as enticing imagery. Consider in-store display and ensure that packs can be stacked on shelves with ease.

01 Client: Pulmuone Wildwood
Design: Shimokochi-Reeves

01

Methodology

Research

Neither the pack shape nor the materials are stipulated in this brief, so it would be valuable not only to research the existing styles of surface graphics in beverage packaging, but also to take time to explore the structures and materials used for various containers. Consider pack construction in other products if you want to follow a more unusual approach; however, it is essential that the packs look as though they contain tea, so you need to understand what visual cues register with consumers to help them recognize a particular product. Look for commonalities of colors, images, patterns, and typefaces that "say" tea. The idea, of course, is not to copy any existing designs, but with packaging in particular, certain visual codes have developed and if a product sits totally outside an expected visual genre, it may not be recognized and therefore may not be purchased. The challenge is to create a pack that combines originality and distinction with the use of an appropriate, acknowledged visual language that consumers can identify easily.

Spend time assessing how designs function within a 3D context; make observations concerning how sides relate to each other and, in particular, the manner in which image and text come together at edges and folds. In some of the inspiring examples shown in this section, the designers have been careful to ensure that information positioned on curved surfaces is legible without any need to rotate the pack.

Exploration and thumbnails

Experiment with a variety of container shapes, considering how more unusual formats will stack on the store shelves. Creating a pack that involves interesting shapes and folds is a challenge that needs to be approached with a degree of dexterity. If this is your first experience of structural packaging, don't to be too ambitious—work primarily with surface graphics by applying designs to an existing pack shape.

Another area for experimentation and analysis is the naming of this tea range. Don't just think about how the name will sound and what it means, but also how it can be interpreted typographically. If you develop a distinctive namestyle, this will have a strong impact on all other design decisions, so you will need to take it into consideration from the very outset of your thumbnail designs.

As with all of the projects in this book, it is important to begin developing thumbnail designs on marker paper: this allows for easy, speedy exploration of a whole range of alternatives. Even at this early stage it is important to view your rough designs in 3D. This might mean simply pasting copies of roughs onto an existing container, or one that has been assembled especially for this role. You can also create roughs by exploring the generation of type- and image-based design detail on-screen. It is often useful to mix hand- and computer-generated visuals to assess the strengths and weaknesses of various design options. When you do assess your design options, stand back, consider solutions in context, and don't forget to obtain a number of unbiased opinions.

02 Client: Fully Loaded Tea
Design: Subplot Design

The design for this tea packaging can be typographically led, illustratively focused, or branded predominantly by the form of the pack. You need to think about all three areas, but, for example, if you think a specific style of illustration would be an effective way of capturing a desired character, then you can use rough illustrations to sketch out your idea and add other necessary information and branding detail later on. Using imagery in this way could be a vital and attractive means of initiating and developing a solution.

These are excellent examples of design being used to create the impression of an indulgent brand. Until comparatively recently, beverage packaging communicated nothing more than the essential product and branding information; now a whole range of tea and coffee brands compete for attention, each promising different benefits.

01 Client: Calistoga Bakery Café
Design: Vrontikis Design Office

Design development
Ideally, at this stage, two or three design concepts should show potential, and it is good practice to be developing a variety of options. Often the viability of a concept won't become clear until it is applied within the context of the entire design. Ideas that appeared the most promising may ultimately turn out to be less successful than those that initially appeared lacking. Always be aware that each individual aspect has a functioning relationship with every element that makes up the packaging solution. Until most of the details from the pack design have been tackled, it is impossible to assess the success of the concept.

01

02/03/04 Client: Fully Loaded Tea
Design: Subplot Design

02

03

04

Completion

The presentation of package designs requires time and dexterity—even the most successful concepts will appear weak and uninviting if the visuals are not made up carefully in 3D form. If you are using an existing container, you can apply computer printouts to the outside; if you are creating an original format and have to construct the pack yourself, it is advisable to use comparatively lightweight card to avoid problems at folds, corners, and joins. For displaying your packaging designs in a print portfolio, mounted photographs of the visuals are the most appropriate option. Online presentation is also a very practical way to display your design solutions. You can upload your work, as a PDF or as separate images, to your own site or to commercial portfolio sites.

The reference material on this spread demonstrates how surface graphics can influence the audience's perception of a product. Virtually all of these examples feature tins and drums of similar proportions, but through the use of very different visual and verbal language the products appear distinct.

01

01 Client: Cafés el Magnífico
Design: Sonsoles Llorens

02 Client: Sans & Sans Fine Tea Merchants
Design: Sonsoles Llorens

Solutions

Project: Tea packaging
Design: Bright Pink

All three visuals include the same photograph of
a tea plantation and have the same design; only the
colorway, along with the name and strapline for the tea,
change. The photograph provides interest in terms of
subject matter, texture, and tone, and complements the
fairly simple typography. As these are purely visuals,
it is perfectly acceptable to use indicative imagery
in place of the photographs that will be used in the
completed solution. Choosing colors that are distinct,
yet work well together, is always a challenge. In this
instance they have been taken from different sides
of the spectrum and although they are not strictly
complementary colors, they are sufficiently close to
be successful. A palette of all hot colors, all tertiary,
all muted, or all primary colors would also be suitable.

"There are very few cases in which packaging's role is to obscure rather than reveal. Nearly all packaging must, at a very quick glance, reveal the nature or contents of the packaging to some degree. It is most important that the designer understands the category they are designing for."

Matthew Clark, Subplot Design

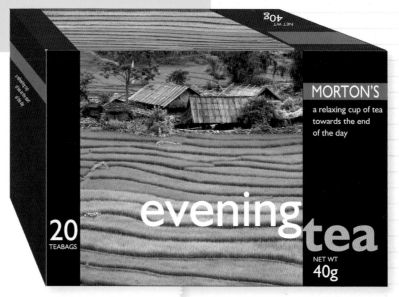

Project: Tea packaging
Design: Bright Pink

Having produced three basically typographic labels for a more unusual form of packaging—tubs—these visuals explore color relationships to find the most appropriate both for individual labels and for the set of three. The designs reflect the names of the teas, with the sun or moon substituted for a letter or part of a letter in each label: the rising sun in the morning, the full afternoon sun, and the moon in the evening sky. Following this, the colors were selected to reflect morning freshness, afternoon brightness, and evening peace, without being too clichéd. The finished labels are displayed on matte black tubs; in all three the word "tea" appears in black to provide a visual link between the label and the tubs. Adding a light border to each label lifts and highlights the circles.

Project: Tea packaging

Design: Bright Pink

It is comparatively easy to create simple illustrative styles and patterns in a number of software programs, or by hand. These decorative curls and leaves bring to mind plants and nature and suggest a certain luxury—that this cup of tea is quite special. These visuals explore typeface and color relationships. In this concept the package for each tea uses two colors; as there are three types of tea, the concept requires six colors that show individuality, yet cohesion. The final concepts for this range are rendered in two colors and black, using flat blocks of color to hold the illustration and type together and also to lead the viewer's eye into and through the information. The colors are all selected from the same side of the spectrum to emphasize that they are part of a range, with black providing continuity. Pale tints in the background avoid empty white spaces and allow for illustration and text to be reversed through.

tea
tea
tea
tea

afternoon
afternoon
afternoon
afternoon
afternoon

"Often fonts with a number of contrasting aspects will work well together, for example, one bold the other light, one italic the other roman, one in all caps and the other in lowercase."

Carolyn Knight and Jessica Glaser, Bright Pink

20
TEABAGS

MORTON'S

a refreshing cup
of tea at the start
of the day
morning
tea

NET WT
40g

a refreshing cup
of tea at the start
of the day

Brief 03

Cosmetics packaging

The brief

Design a range of packaging for new cosmetics brand Fred & Miah

The brief explained

Target market

The target market is male and female users of cosmetics and beauty products, aged between 18 and 35, with an interest in cultural diversity and contemporary style and design. Purchasers will have a high disposable income, follow trends in fashion, and be comfortable spending a considerable percentage of their money on luxury items including leisure, travel, and pampering.

Requirements

Apply designs to at least four different items, one of which should be a liquid-based product, such as shampoo or toner. Be sure that selected items reflect a diverse range of products. Each design must be resealable while also having regard for hygiene and ease of use. There are no color restrictions or structural limitations other than those posed by the practicalities of commercial manufacture. Develop a brand identity for Fred & Miah that has the scope to be applied effectively to all products in the range, ensuring appeal to both male and female consumers.

01

01 Client: Avalon Natural Products
Design: Shimokochi-Reeves

02 Project: Cosmetics packaging
Design: Rajiv Chada

Methodology

Research

There is a vast array of beauty products on the shelves of department stores. Before embarking on any design ideas for this project, take a notepad to the perfume, aftershave, and cosmetics sections of your local mall or store and record, in words and sketches, significant styles of competitor products. Note the colors, typefaces, shapes, and patterns that characterize each brand. Remember, two key aspects of the brief concern the intended target market and contemporary style. Your research in the cosmetics departments should focus on the range of visual language that "says" this product is for pampering, hygiene, or cleanliness. This will give you an idea of what scope you have for pushing boundaries in your design. You should also look into the visual languages of different cultures, and at current fashions and trends in graphics. There's no need to limit yourself to packaging—work within any genre will give you valuable insights. Essentially, research is not an exercise in copying existing ideas, but more a process of accumulating knowledge that informs and influences future design work. While the brief does not specify any costs of the products within the Fred & Miah range, it is important that you decide whether the items will be upmarket and command premium prices, or whether they will be more everyday consumables, as this will affect final designs.

Exploration and thumbnails

You could begin experimenting by drawing the product name in a number of different typefaces, in upper- and lowercase, and in a mix of both. Use the arrangement of the letters and letterspacing to create character. Although it can be hard to replicate a variety of production techniques and materials, try a selection of mark-making implements on unusual surfaces. Combinations of drawing tools and of matte and gloss, textured and smooth surfaces can create really exciting effects. Experiment with the shapes of containers; take existing vessels that are typical of other kinds of products and make strategic use of symbolic beauty product graphics. Clearly, there are conventions to be observed and consumer expectations to be met, but don't be too inhibited by these at the start of the design process—allow your concepts to be innovative and imaginative. Ideas can usually be "tamed" if they have become rather wild and unrealistic; it is always more difficult to inject excitement into mundane designs.

Although your initial thumbnails may be 2D, your designs will benefit if you attempt 3D maquettes at a fairly early stage—it is really helpful to get an impression of how a design is going to function in 3D form from the outset. They can be made out of paper providing it isn't too flimsy, and the models don't need to be full-size. Designing can be a little like juggling in that, at any one time, you need to keep a number of design elements in the air! For this project you need to create a namestyle for Fred & Miah, and along with that you must consider supporting graphics such as colors and patterns, and print techniques. You also need to choose the shapes of containers for four different items in the product range. It is imperative that all elements have individuality, yet cohesion as a group. While exploring lots of alternatives, you need to juggle typefaces, colors, materials, and constructions in order to ensure that all elements work well together. They will all impact on one another not only from a practical point of view, but also in terms of visual cohesion. For example, if a rounded typeface is selected, any graphic marks or patterns that are used should reflect its inherent curves, and the shapes of the containers should be predominantly rounded.

Design development

Your experimentation and exploration should produce at least one concept with potential for further development. This concept must be refined to ensure that it functions satisfactorily across the whole project. The significance of the developmental stage of any design should not be underestimated—it is just as important as coming up with a good idea. In fact, many excellent ideas are lost because the creative process is not continued right through to the application of designs. With this project there is the opportunity to develop a concept in four ways, as four different packs have to be produced. The ideal result is that all four look as though they belong to the same range, but also allow some scope in applying the brand image.

One of the best methods for attaining the kind of continuity and variety required in this context is to reverse the roles of different design elements. Color reversal can be extremely effective. For example, if one pack is predominantly red with white type and image reversed through, you could give another pack a white background with red type and image. Priorities of scale and emphasis can also be changed, and if a textured quality is part of the design, this can be used for different elements. In developing an idea, review and cross-examine it regularly to make sure it maintains the recognizable look of the brand.

Development also includes the translation of your rough visuals into more accurate computer-generated versions of complete packs. These can be applied to flat structural designs, parts of flat structural designs, or to individual sides.

01

Your reference material for this project should be gathered from a wide variety of sources: store shelves, the bathroom cabinet, even the local museum.

01 Client: Essie Cosmetics
Design: Stormhouse Partners

02 Client: Essie Cosmetics

Design: Stormhouse Partners

03 Client: Jan Stuart

Design: Stormhouse Partners

04 Client:

Gianna Rose

Design: Sayles

Graphic Design

Completion

Set time aside to make up the four packs accurately, ready to be photographed. Try to avoid two cut edges of computer printouts meeting on the corners without any overlap, as that will make it almost impossible to avoid a gap; use spray adhesive to glue them to containers smoothly. You may find it expedient to mount the printouts on flat, lightweight card; if you do this, avoid any overlap and make sure the printouts butt up precisely. Score the folds on the inside of the card before securing the flaps with double-sided tape. If you can, print out your design on a single sheet of heavier-weight material that can be cut, scored, and folded straight into 3D form. Mount photographs of finished 3D visuals on medium-weight, neutral-colored card to display in your print portfolio. Online presentation is also a practical way to display your designs. You can upload your work, as a PDF or as separate images, to your own site or to commercial portfolio sites.

Solutions

Cosmetics packaging

Design: Lotte Hammergren Andresen

Lotte Hammergren Andresen designed dynamic, triangular packs with white embossed type contrasting subtly with white containers. Her typographic choices build on the triangular theme with certain letterforms echoing this shape. The tall pack is made up of two distinct containers, one for fragrance Fred and the other for fragrance Miah. These two packs meet in the middle with the aid of a star-shaped locking device. Lotte also designed two smaller triangular packs for cream, and these repeat the simple typographic styling.

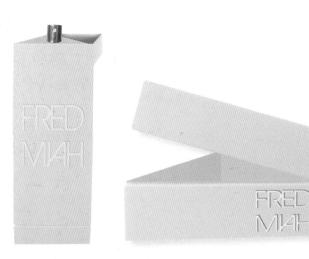

"The printing options open to packaging designers range from high-end rotogravure to flexo to litho-laminate to silkscreen, and the substrates vary from carton to board stock to glass to labels to shrink-film. Knowing what techniques and materials are available allows you to design with intelligence."

Carolyn Knight and Jessica Glaser, Bright Pink

Project: Cosmetics packaging
Design: Caroline Kruse Pettersson

This solution for Fred & Miah cosmetics is based on variations on a theme of circles. Colored beads are used cleverly in every pack, with circular symbols, rounded letterforms, and a texture made from overlapping circles playing a dominant role in the concept behind this design. In some of the packs the transparency of the product is an integral element, allowing you a pleasing view of strings of colored beads suspended within the fragrance. Beads are used to form mnemonic handles and an unusual element within the design for a lip-balm key fob. The computer-generated visuals use a mix of photography and image manipulation.

fred miah
moisturizer

fred miah
fragrance for her

fred miah
fragrance for him

fred miah

ingredients:
alcohol denat. fred&miah fragrance(parfum), water/ aqua/eau, butylphenyl methylpropional, hydroxylsohexyl 3-cyclohexene carboxaldehyde, alpha-isomethyl ionone, geraniol, linalool, hydroxycitronellal, citronellol, bht, isoeugenol, methyl 2-octynoate, tetrasodium edta butyl methoxydibenzoylmethane, ethylhexyl methoxycinnamate, ethylhexyl salicylate <8LN97/1>

fredandmiah.com

© FRED & MIAH COSMETICS, DIST. LONDON, U.K. W1X 38Q MADE IN U.K. 81WN

3.4 FL.OZ./.LIQ./50 ml ℮

Project: Cosmetics packaging
Design: Catherine Tønnessen

Typefaces are often selected with a view to reflecting the shapes or forms found in a design. In this instance, however, Catherine Tønnessen has chosen to go with contrast: she has complemented her circular containers with a dynamic namestyle that is very angular and composed entirely of straight lines.

Project: Cosmetics packaging
Design: Alex Goodier

Male and female icons play an important role in this striking design, with the two figures joining to take the place of the ampersand between Fred & Miah. The figures are also used in isolation and wrap attractively round the corners of the packs. Bright pink and black boxes contrast with white product containers to create a simple, yet eye-catching design.

Project: Cosmetics packaging
Design: Aneesa Iqbal

The Fred & Miah namestyle is interpreted using two contrasting typefaces that emphasize the male and female appeal of the brand. A lightweight sans serif face combines with fine rules to represent masculinity; a more floral, ornate face represents femininity. Aneesa Iqbal links the sides of the boxes with extending rules and uses color reversal in the packaging to create two distinct, yet related aspects for the brand.

"The reversal of colors is a successful design option that maintains consistency and gives a sense of belonging to a particular brand or style, while allowing for individuality and scope."

Carolyn Knight and Jessica Glaser, Bright Pink

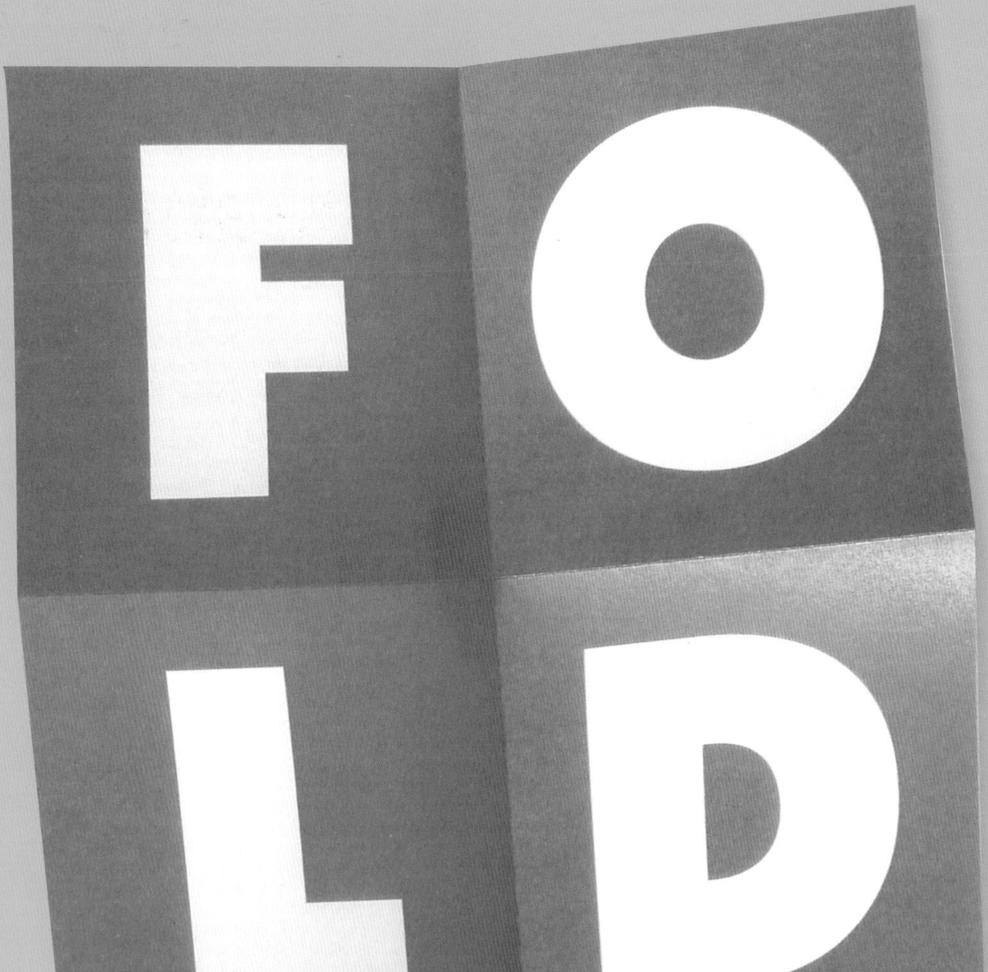
FOLD

Section 02
Visual identity & branding

Visual identity and branding share many characteristics. In its simplest form, visual identity design can be described as the development and application of a distinct logotype and/or symbol that makes a company or organization recognizable. Branding is the establishment of value and status for a unique product, service, or organization through the careful application of an identity.

In both instances appropriate visual elements—typefaces, groupings, and color—need to be brought together cohesively to represent the distinct character of the brand. What makes a brand a brand is a namestyle that captures and communicates this unique character, and it is that which makes it a highly marketable entity.

Establishing a brand is likely to involve some considerable advertising and promotion, in a large variety of forms and locations, as an audience's familiarity with and impression of an identity plays a significant role in the development of a successful brand.

Corporate identity involves not only a visible namestyle or symbol, but also the creation and practice of an organizational culture. Corporate identity guidelines include both behavioral directives and notes on dress and uniforms. Corporate identities can create a strong sense of belonging for employees and customers alike.

01 Client: Lily
Design: Oded Ezer

13 -15 May 2008
NEC Birmingham

FOR **ALL** YOUR FM NEEDS

12 - 15 May 2008
HALL **6** NEC Birmingham

Consistency is important in the application of identity and branding designs, but this should not lead to monotony. Matthew Clark of Subplot Design says "Consistency is great, and most clients and designers have been taught that it is the end goal. I have been in many initial meetings where the client specifically requests that their new identity be 'consistent.' But without intelligence, a solid brand platform, a breakthrough idea or unique design ... does consistency get you anywhere? Consistency should not be ignored, but the goal is for big, smart, and breakthrough ideas that elevate our clients above their competition. So nail that first. Then go to work on keeping it consistent."

The creation of an identity involves combining such elements as selected typefaces, colors, compositional relationships, and spatial distribution. You can create a successful identity and brand by keeping at least one of these elements fixed and introducing variety through the others. If you maintain a palette of brand colors through all the designs, the identity can remain strong with a surprising variety of typefaces, typographic systems, and groupings.

02 Client: Protection and Management Services
Design: Début

The right balance of consistency and flexibility can be difficult to define. For example, if a namestyle or symbol is always used at the same size and in the same position, this can result in a range of disappointingly bland solutions, but if it is applied differently in every context the design cohesion can be lost and solutions will not be perceived as belonging to the same group. As with so much design there are no definable rules or regulations. Observation and experience will help you make such judgments and over time you will begin to develop an almost intuitive, professionally reasoned knowledge of these subjects.

In Matthew Clark's words, "A strong identity system balances an approach to identity creation and regulation where rigidity (necessary to enforce compliance) is balanced with flexibility (to cover all the unforeseen applications that crop up over time). When developing our identity systems, we begin the process with a large brand audit and create a map of every touchpoint and material that the client currently has or anticipates needing. This gives us a firm scope for the project, and a target to aim for when developing the rules of the identity. The way you justify type on a business card has a bearing on how you set type on the corporate brochure ... but your system may have a more flexible set of design principles where corporate stationery

01 Client: Badalona City Council
Design: Sonsoles Llorens

and consumer point-of-sale may have very different principles because of the very different audiences and formats. Navigating these nuances and balancing rigidity with flexibility is what separates the strong from the weak identity system."

Developing a visual identity palette will help you address flexibility and scope. A visual identity palette includes not just a namestyle, but a whole range of visual elements including texture and pattern. Typographic systems, relationships of scale, spatial relationships, use of color, style of imagery, art direction, use and character of materials, and style of language are all available as design choices. You can introduce flexibility and scope through changes in any one of these elements. Establishing an identity palette makes it easier to introduce such variety while maintaining strong visual connections and links across various applications.

Very often the colors used for a visual identity will need to expand to accommodate subdivisions or extensions of a brand, so it can be useful for an identity palette to include a number of colors, each with a definable association. The use of tonal variations and/or appropriately colored versions of patterns and textures is an excellent way of extending the color aspect of an identity palette. It may not always be necessary to add a completely new color—the use of a tint can give a brand or identity added breadth, meaning, and interest.

02/03 Client: Badalona City Council
Design: Sonsoles Llorens

03

01

01/02 Client: Kasian
Design: Subplot Design

The interpretation of imagery, whether photographic or illustrative, can be a key element in an identity palette. The subject matter, depth of field, style of mark-making, form of cropping, proportion and shape of image box, and use of color are all possible areas of focus for creating distinctive stylistic themes. Color within imagery is an underused tool. Even where photography is the most appropriate form of illustration, brand colors can be incorporated. If the brand or identity colors are vibrant green and muted grey, items that pick up those colors within the photograph can be featured, or the image can be manipulated as a duotone or single-color halftone.

Compositional characteristics can form a distinctive part of an identity palette. The configuration of an organization's namestyle can influence the manner in which you bring imagery and type together. For example, a namestyle that is closely leaded and tracked and staggered across a number of lines might suggest presenting a group of images or sections of text in the same way. Spatial distribution can also contribute key characteristics to an identity. In general a busy design suggests a very different personality from a more restrained layout with a luxurious, extravagant use of space.

02

What do we mean when we say we make "Craft Beer"?

{ _Stefan Tobler_ }
BREWMASTER STEFAN TOBLER

Quality. Best Ingredients. Freshness. Full taste. It's about the spirit of small batches made for local customers. It's about the discovery of different styles of beer and the care, attention and knowledge that goes into brewing each and every one of them. To us at the Okanagan Spring Brewery, our passion for the craft of brewing is the very reason we exist.

03

03/04 Okanagan
Spring Brewery
Design: Subplot
Design

Different kinds of industries, organizations, and markets often have particular visual codes that are synonymous with their areas of expertise and interest. While it is essential to acknowledge any subject-specific code, if a design is to be fresh, innovative, and successful, it must also be distinctive. Gregory Paone of Paone Design Associates suggests that "identity design endeavors to communicate the essence of an idea by the most simple, yet powerful means. If those means tap into a universal vocabulary which best describes the characteristics of an industry or service, then the designer will communicate to the widest audience. If, however, the designer is able to create an equally engaging graphic language that is unorthodox in its connection to the subject, one could argue that this approach is valid because it constitutes a fresh interpretation."

Establishing the brand values that need to be communicated to an audience is fundamental to your understanding of whether recognized visual codes should be adopted or challenged. If a client wishes to benefit from the reliable reputation of a wider industry, it is important that the visual codes of that industry are clearly acknowledged and in some respects overtly included in the identity you develop. However, if it is more valuable to communicate the contemporary nature of a company or product, you should look to originating a fresh approach. Earl Gee of Gee + Chung Design says, "At the start of any identity project it is essential for the designer to avoid any preconceptions about a client category and keep an open mind. They should conduct a thorough visual audit of the brands that exist within the client's specific industry and which the target audience may encounter. The purpose is to learn what symbols, styles, and colors are commonly used within the client's industry, and what is appropriate for the client's audience. Armed with the knowledge of what exists and what is expected, the designer can then decide how to truly differentiate his client."

Glossary

alignment the arrangement of image and text in a design, typically from a left, right, central, top, or bottom axis

ascender the part of a lowercase letter that rises above the x-height of the font, as in the letters b, d, f, h, k, l, and t

baseline the imaginary horizontal line upon which the main body of letters in a block of text sits

brand identity the visual image the public has of a product

branding the application of a distinct logotype and/or symbol to make a company or organization recognizable, along with the marketing that imbues the company with a personality

condensed letterforms letters in which the set widths of the characters are narrower than in a standard typeface

corporate identity the visible style of a company (including the namestyle and/ or symbol) together with its organizational and behavioral culture

depth of field the distance between the nearest and furthest points in a photo that appear in focus; with a short depth of field only a small area of an image will be in focus; with a long depth of field the whole photograph will be in focus

descender the part of the letterform that dips below the baseline

elements of design the building blocks of design: color, shape, size, space, line, value, and texture

expanded letterforms letters in which the set widths of the characters are wider than in a standard typeface

graphic language visual meaning created by the coming together of graphic elements rather than words

hierarchy the arrangement of elements planned so as to guide viewers through them in a specific order

identity palette the visual elements that come together to form an identity; an identity palette can be used much like an artist's palette, with elements selected in various combinations

kerning the space between individual letterforms

logo/logotype a distinctive visual character created by the design of the letters that constitute a product name; a namestyle

marker paper specialist thin paper with a coating that prevents marker pens from bleeding through

mark-making the process of applying pen or pencil to paper; the character of marks made by different implements or technological effects

namestyle see logo/logotype

paper stock a particular kind and weight of paper; the paper to be printed on

signposted character the distinctive characteristics that distinguish a company's identity

strapline descriptive line of text that sums up the unique selling point(s) of a product

symbol a distinctive image or mark that represents a product; generally works with a namestyle

system (design system) the criteria used to organize different elements in relation to each other to form a considered whole

target market the audience to whom a design is intended to appeal

thumbnails comparatively small rough visuals that incorporate sufficient detail and accuracy to be of value for decision-making

tracking the letterspacing applied across a line of text

typographic weight the thickness or thinness of letterforms creating different degrees of bold, medium, or light type

visual audit an evaluation of visual elements

visual code/visual cue visual element or group of elements that have a definite connotation due to frequency of use in similar situations

visual identity the application of a distinct logotype and/or symbol that makes a company or organization recognizable

x-height the height of the lowercase letters, excluding ascenders and descenders

Reading list

100% European Graphic Design Portfolio
various

The Art of Looking Sideways
Alan Fletcher

Branding: From Brief to Finished Solution
Mono Design

Graphis Design Annual
Martin Pederson

Graphis Letterhead
Martin Pederson

Letterhead & Logo Design 9
MINE

Lingua Universalis: Global Wordless Understanding
Heinrich Paravicini and Johannes Plass

Logo-Art: Innovation in Logo Design
Charlotte Rivers

Los Logos 4
Hendrick Hellige and Robert Klanten

Naked Thoughts: Diaries, Notebooks + Sketchbooks
Marc A. Valli, Mairi Duthie, Matt Willey, and Zoë Bather

On Brand
Wally Olins

A Smile in the Mind: Witty Thinking in Graphic Design
Beryl McAlhone and David Stuart

The Typographer's Guide to the Galaxy
Oded Ezer

Equipment

- Scalpel
- Marker paper
- Tracing paper
- Pencils
- Markers/colored pencils
- Ruler
- Set square
- Typeface reference
- Cutting mat
- Double-sided tape
- Low-tack adhesive tape
- Adhesive tape
- Matte finish invisible adhesive tape
- Spray adhesive
- Lightweight card
- Professional color matching reference
- Computer/software

Brief 01

Stationery

01 ▷

The brief

**Design a range of stationery for Smile Style
Dental Care Practice using the namestyle supplied**

The brief explained

Target market

The target audience of Smile Style Dental Care
stationery is not just existing Smile Style clients, but
also potential new clients. It has sufficient income
to afford private dental care, and values top-quality
treatment. The target market is informed individuals
and families with a high regard for good health.

Requirements

Graphic designers often have to originate solutions
using established identities or other pre-existing
elements. This is one such project. Use the supplied
namestyle, strapline, and color scheme to design a
letterhead, compliments slip, and business card for
Smile Style Dental Care. The designs should exploit
both the creative and the practical possibilities that
are "signposted" by the design approach of the
existing Smile Style brand.

02 ▷

01/02 Client: Kasian
Design: Subplot Design

Smile **STYLE**

DENTAL CARE CENT

Methodology

Research

There are many opportunities for researching comprehensive ranges of stationery, both online and in books, not to mention the real examples of printed stationery that come in the post. Take time to analyze relevant examples. Pay attention to the detail included on each item of the range: look at the space and importance accorded this detail, and examine other aspects including positioning, scale, and grouping of elements.

As part of your research, look at your options for different paper stocks and note which ones work best to complement and reinforce the style of this identity. Think about how this stationery will be used and received. How will a letterhead fold into an envelope? How might it be filed, and will it be photocopied? The answers to these questions will have a vital impact on the layout of elements in a finished letterhead design.

A stationery range is also likely to include items such as business cards, compliments slips, and notepaper—it is important that each individual item be perceived as part of the one set. Many aspects will come into play in achieving this, including cohesion of typestyle and typographic systems, uniformity of color, and the use and consistency of orientation, grouping, and positioning.

Business cards are likely to be among the smallest items you have worked on, and this will bring fresh challenges relating specifically to scale, format, and legibility. With very little space to work in, you need to find the best, most effective way to group information, while remaining faithful to the recognized systems that are integral to the identity.

Every logo and namestyle has its own distinctive characteristics; these characteristics are referred to as being "signposted." Individuality can come from aspects such as color; the use of a distinct symbol or shape; relationships of scale; positioning and orientation; or a significant combination and use of fonts. Recognizing well-defined characteristics such as these helps to flag up areas of the design that will provide you with good design options to extend the scope of the identity and its applications while maintaining a specific close connection with the design decisions made by the designer of the original logo.

Analyze the Smile Style mark in detail. It is based on the typefaces Clarendon and Futura, and printed in two Pantone inks—PMS 493 and PMS 645. These inks can be used as tints in order to extend the design possibilities of the identity. Look for shapes and relationships to help provide reasoned indicators for subsequent design decisions.

Exploration and thumbnails

Having spent time researching other stationery designs and considering how these will be used and read, record design possibilities for the Smile Style stationery design. Always render your thumbnails in proportion to the finished size of each individual item: there is no point spending time working on a design that is not in scale with, and therefore won't represent the positioning of elements within, the final design. While working through alternatives, think about ways of extending the design possibilities presented by this identity. Positioning the namestyle in the usual top right-hand corner of stationery might disappoint; a more unusual placement of an identity is certain to captivate and intrigue an audience. Consider the use of shifts in color priority, and think about the possibilities for reversing certain elements through a background color or tint.

Design development

Once you have worked through various possible solutions, select a few to develop at full size on-screen. You can enlarge your thumbnail designs on a photocopier or with a scanner and use these images as a plan to help you translate the designs accurately. Remember to print out computer-generated design options at full size as you work up the designs so that you can check relationships of scale and spacing. Consider how correspondence might be laid out on the letterhead and how this arrangement might impact on ways of folding the design to ensure a comfortable fit in an envelope. Canvas the opinion of colleagues and discuss the alternatives being explored, as this will help you refine your solutions.

01

Variety with consistency is the key to the successful development of a range of stationery, and the sets shown here, and on the following page, illustrate this point.

01 Client: Dove Entertainments
Design: boing!

02

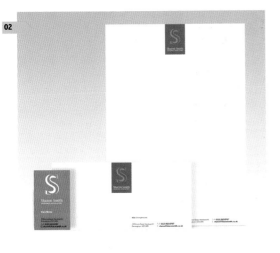

04 Client: Give Something Back International
Design: Gee + Chung Design

04

02 Client: Sharon Smith Upholstery
Design: boing!

03 Client: Net Sage
Design: Ames Bros

03

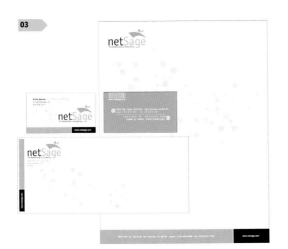

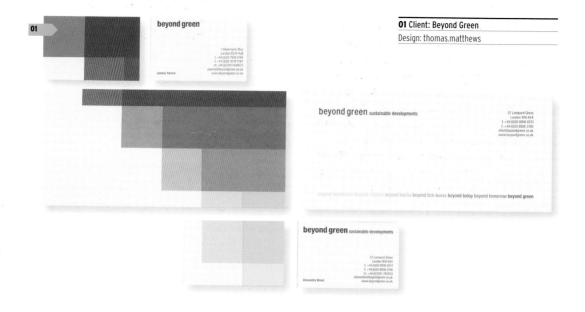

Completion

It is a good idea to present letterhead designs with a letter in place to demonstrate the functionality of the design. Print out the final stationery range on your selected stock—this should have a texture or surface that fits the character of Smile Style. For your print portfolio, mount your final designs on a contrasting, medium-weight presentation board. Online portfolios can also be a very practical way to display your design solutions, whether as a PDF or as separate digital images. Designs can be uploaded to personal or commercial portfolio sites.

03

An element of humor has been included in all of these samples, leaving the viewer amused and uplifted. Such memorable designs have the added advantage of establishing an emotional connection that can benefit the company concerned.

01

01/02 Client: Banana Split

Design: Fivefootsix

02

03 Client: Film London

Design: ArthurSteenHorneAdamson

04 Client: Lisa Desforges

Design: Fivefootsix

Graham Gill Carpets Established 1965
24 West Street Boston Lincolnshire PE21 8QH
Telephone and Fax 01205 365 350
www.grahamgillcarpets.co.uk

05 Client: Graham Gill

Design: Fivefootsix

Jane Desforges

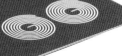

Solutions

Project: Stationery design
Design: Bright Pink

As the Smile Style namestyle has been provided for this brief, the student work uses the namestyle for Bright Pink Communications Design in order to give guidance for appropriate ways of working without providing actual solutions.

The first concept for the stationery looks at introducing a block of pink that bleeds off one or more edges of each item, with the words "communications design" in white reversed through the black bars. The pink block has been applied in two ways: one has the pink running right across the bottom and bleeding off on three sides, the other has a section of pink coming in from the top. While both have potential, the most consistent solution, with the letterhead, compliments slip, and business card all adopting the same treatment, would be to have pink panels that either bleed off on three edges, or bleed off on just one.

"It is important to include variety in a range of stationery, but every item should look as though it belongs to the set as a whole. Very often it is the manner in which elements come together that needs to remain constant—flexibility can often be injected into other areas of the design."

Carolyn Knight and Jessica Glaser, Bright Pink

JESSICA GLASER
Partner

LAPLEY STUDIO
LAPLEY, STAFFORD ST19 9JS
TELEPHONE: 01785 841601
FAX: 01785 841401
studio@brightpinkdesign.co.uk

Project: Stationery design
Design: Bright Pink

This design idea exploits a lively juxtaposition of
the letters that form the words "Bright Pink," allowing
some of the serifs at the edges to bleed off. Within
each version both continuity and variety are achieved.
The horizontals and verticals in the logo provide
excellent alignment points for the address detail and
the black dots on the "i"s introduce a second color,
which is reflected in all supporting text. This concept is
particularly successful in using the dynamic of contrast
of scale to bring the design to life. Note that in these
versions, as the bar either side of "Bright Pink" is not
included in the namestyle, the text contained in those
bars—communications design—has been added to the
address detail.

Project: Stationery design
Design: Bright Pink

In many respects this concept for the Bright Pink stationery is the most straightforward, however, it still achieves interesting contrasts of scale and variety through color reversals. The letterhead is comparatively formal in layout, with pink letterforms and black bars; the compliments slip employs the same color combination, but at a considerably larger size; and the business card introduces black letters and pink bars. In order to create the change of scale, both the business card and the compliments slip take the complete logo up to the full width, however, while this leaves just enough room for the necessary text on the business card, it leaves no room for a personal note on the compliments slip.

Project: Stationery design
Design: Bright Pink

In this concept the bars containing the words
"communications design" are extended to become
thick rules that bleed off left and right. When
"communications design" is set in pink reversed
through the black, it gives the appearance that the logo
is sitting on the pink bars. The two variations for the
compliments slip explore different color relationships;
although the bars have not been extended, by making
the item portrait with the namestyle reaching the full
width, the effect is the same. The business card from
the previous concept could be a part of this set.

BRIGHT PINK
COMMUNICATIONS DESIGN
LAPLEY STUDIO
LAPLEY, STAFFORD ST19 9JS
TELEPHONE: 01785 841601
FAX: 01785 841401
studio@brightpinkdesign.co.uk

PARTNERS:
CAROLYN KNIGHT & JESSICA GLASER
VAT NO: 715006175

"When looking to apply a logo to stationery or any
other context, it is essential to analyze every aspect
of its form and take the opportunity to explore as many
appropriate and relevant developments as possible."

Jeff Leak, boing!

Brief 02

Namestyle

The brief

Design a namestyle for an international newsgathering organization called Informant

The brief explained

Target market

The target market is decision-makers in the business community and in particular, journalists working in print, screen, and radio. Informant should be positioned as a reliable and well-informed source of impartial current affairs reporting in the realms of high-quality business-to-business consultancy.

Requirements

The design must function in both two-color and single-color versions, and be legible at both large and small scale, in a variety of contexts. Use typography to interpret the name "Informant." Develop a unique and significant namestyle that conveys the essence of Informant's business activity. The namestyle must be visually interesting, clearly legible, impactful, and indicative of Informant's impeccable reputation for high-quality journalism and newsgathering.

01 Client: Film London
Design: ArthurSteenHorneAdamson

Methodology

Research

There are many books and websites dedicated to showcasing logotypes and namestyles and it is definitely worth taking a look at some of these inspirational resources. Investigate examples of logos designed specifically for newsgathering organizations and associated companies. It is crucial to examine, in detail, how these designs convey the essence of a company's activity: how have the designers communicated the activity of newsgathering, how is the topic of current affairs captured, and the reputation and longevity of the organization conveyed? Has a specific color palette been adopted across these logos, and have any similar typefaces been used? Take note of any visual characteristics that have become synonymous with newsgathering. Often the designer's task is to generate concepts that not only possess originality, but also appear to "belong" to the appropriate genre.

As part of your research it's a good idea to look at the use of two-color print, as this project specifies that solutions should function in both two-color and single-color versions. Many innovative and unexpected effects can be achieved when working within what, initially, might seem like very restricted parameters. These limitations can prove to be a stimulating and invigorating challenge that prompts the graphic designer to experiment in a manner that is outside their usual comfort zone. When considering the use of color, remember that the Informant namestyle would ultimately have to function effectively in the contexts of both print and screen.

After analyzing existing namestyles and associated identities, consider the typographic nature of this design in more detail. What are the shapes and attributes of the letterforms that make up the name "Informant?" How many curved, angled, horizontal, or vertical marks make up these letterforms? Is there an unusual individual letter or a repetitive, memorable combination of letterforms that could be developed to provide a distinct and suitable assertion of reputation and character for Informant? Some namestyles use substituted marks that have meaning in their own right, and that are also recognizable as letterforms, or groups of letterforms, that reinforce the quality and reputation of an organization.

02 Client: Love & Co. Café
Design: Simon Winter Design

02

03 Client: Fit Clinic
Design: Simon Winter Design

03

Exploration and thumbnails

Commence thumbnails by rendering the letters of the name "Informant." Experiment to see what the name looks like in lowercase, uppercase, and a mix of the two. Also, give careful consideration to any possible advantages, disadvantages, and consequences of using serif or sans-serif typefaces. Using sheets of marker or layout paper, trace through and experiment with various combinations. In addition to different cases, try mixing typefaces, weights, and scales.

Explore alternative, feasible alignments. The most obvious manner of positioning letterforms is simply to sit them side by side on the same baseline, but take time to assess the shapes and character of the letterforms that comprise the company name: are there any other possible alignments that can be made? For example, can relationships be made between the height of crossbars, the top of x-heights, the top of ascenders, or the bottom of descenders? Exploring choices in this manner can open up avenues for creating exciting and meaningful visual relationships.

Experimenting with color combinations and tonal variations can help you add emphasis to or lessen the impact of specific areas of a namestyle. An easy way to check that a two-color design also functions effectively in a single color is to photocopy a rough in black-and-white—any potential tonal problems will instantly become apparent. Working with a limited color palette is a surprisingly stimulating exercise. Careful mixes of color can produce some unexpected and very helpful new shades. Of course, in a print context, working with Pantone specials can, for the most part, ensure color accuracy. Don't overlook the possibility of using the background color as a contrasting shade to add to the character of an identity or to add stress to a design.

01 The Duke of Edinburgh's Award
Design: ArthurSteenHorneAdamson

Design development

Having produced a range of initial designs, now is the time to develop solutions with the aid of a computer. With namestyles that incorporate relatively few letterforms, the details and character of the individual letters become very apparent and significant. As a result, the interpretation of visuals and selection of actual typefaces creates the most meaningful impact upon a finished design. It is important not only to assess the general character of your mark-making within roughs, but also to consider visual details such as relationships of scale, inter-character spacing, and whether your individual letterforms are in any way condensed or expanded. Careful comparison of the weights indicated within

02 Fold
Design: Sheaff Dorman Purins

thumbnail designs, with a variety of weights available in desired styles of typefaces, will also help you achieve the best, most successful and visually truthful match.

As with all solutions that have a possible print application, it is important to assess designs during the development stage by studying printouts. As the namestyle for Informant is likely to be applied to a variety of items, it is vital that the finished design functions in an assortment of sizes, from the small scale of a business card to the larger sizes needed for signage or promotional designs.

Completion

Your final design should be presented in both single- and two-color versions. Although this project does not stipulate precise applications, think about possible alternatives such as one small-scale use (for example, on an item of stationery) and one larger-scale piece. Mount your final visuals carefully on medium-weight presentation board, ready for display in your print portfolio. Online presentation can also be a very practical way to display your design solutions, whether as a PDF or as separate digital images. Designs can be uploaded to personal or commercial portfolio sites.

A namestyle is a purely typographic mark that involves the manipulation and arrangement of letterforms to create an individual visual representation of a company, organization, service, or product. The examples on this spread are all very different from one another and demonstrate the infinite scope available with this project.

01 Client: no commission, design pitch
Design: Simon Winter Design

02 Client: Film London
Design: ArthurSteenHorneAdamson

01

02

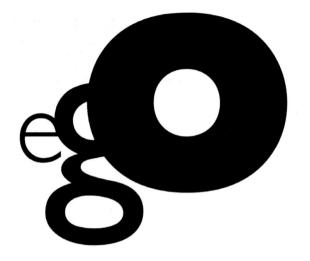

03 Client: Ego
Design: Oded Ezer

04 Client: Hemming Morse
Design: Vrontikis Design Office

05 Client: Brawer & Hauptman Architects
Design: Paone Design Associates

HEMMING MORSE, INC.

CERTIFIED PUBLIC ACCOUNTANTS
LITIGATION & FORENSIC CONSULTANTS

Brawer & Hauptman Architects

Composition, color, mark-making, and change of weight are the
common design elements that run through the examples on this page.
All of these aspects are used to convey pertinent meaning
and association.

01

Si.
Swedish Institute

02

global.○
actio○
sch○○ls

03

01 Client: Swedish Institute
Design: BankerWessel

02 Client: ActionAid
Design: thomas.matthews

03 Client: Wint & Kidd
Design: Fivefootsix

WINT
&
KIDD

FORUM
WEITERBILDUNG
KANTON**B**ERN

FORUM
WEITERBILDUNG
KANTON**B**ERN

04 Client: Forum Weiterbildung
Design: Lorenzo Geiger

SƎSɹƎʌıᗡ IDÉES

05 Client: Idées Diverses
Design: Lorenzo Geiger

BOSTON PARTNERS
IN EDUCATION

06 Client: Boston Partners in Education
Design: Sheaff Dorman Purins

Solutions

Project: Namestyle
Design: Bright Pink

These concepts explore the use of upper- and lowercase letterforms to tease out any meaningful links with communication, information, and news. Red and black are familiar newspaper colors and are therefore appropriate to start the work. Where "Informant" has been split into red and black parts to emphasize the four letters that make up "info," the remaining black letters do not make sense, so this treatment is not successful.

Enlarging letters in the center of a word is borrowed from old blockbuster movie titles and is intended to give significance and grandeur to the company. Its weakness, apart from appearing a little dated, is that the "O" and "M" are very different in character and width, so the visual symmetry required is not possible.

The hand-rendered thumbnail that emphasizes the "i" for "information" is visually interesting and has all the right connotations. A lowercase "i" is the international symbol for "information." It is always lowercase, but the typeface can vary, so the main focus is on finding an "i" that complements the rest of the word. It should catch the eye and lead the reader through the namestyle.

While red and black are appropriate colors, they are perhaps too predictable, so it is important to try out other options. The namestyle has to work in black-and-white—some of these visuals show selected colors translated into grayscale to see whether the logo will work when printed in single color, or when photocopied in black-and-white.

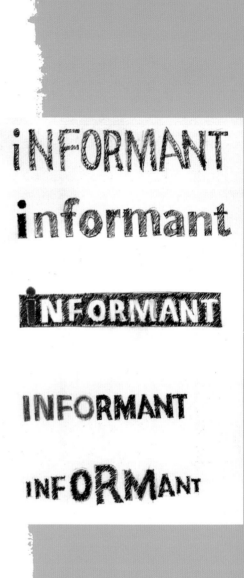

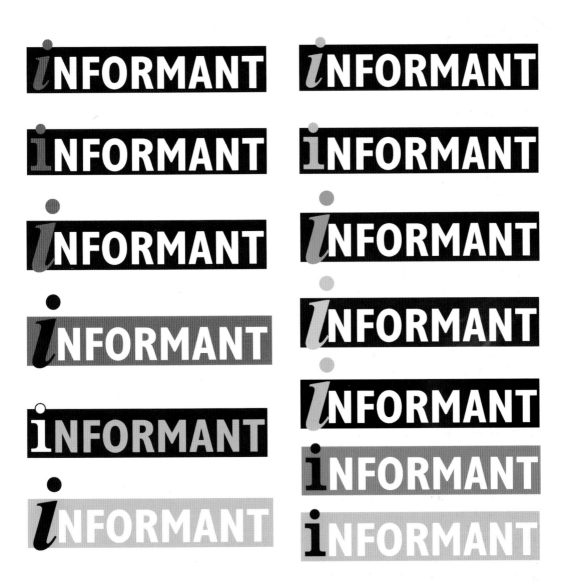

"When a namestyle is intended to be read as a whole and is broken up by a color change, or by any other kind of manipulation such as change of weight or typeface, both sections should make sense separately as well as together."

Carolyn Knight and Jessica Glaser, Bright Pink

Project: Namestyle
Design: Bright Pink

These sketches are developments of a speech-bubble concept. The computer versions explore italic fonts and weights to capture a sense of immediacy, and lowercase letters to create a feeling of informality.

The letterforms other than the "f," which is extended into a swash that is suggestive of a speech bubble, are examined in both roman and italic versions. In all instances the letterspacing is controlled with careful visual judgments.

Where the "o" is replaced with a speech bubble, the contrast in color and scale is distinctive and dynamic, though there is a chance that the speech bubble will be mistaken for a "Q." Because the yellow is lighter in tone than the reds, the overlapping letters do not merge with the speech bubble, so this version is likely to be more successful.

"I am a massive believer in customizing typefaces for final logomarks. While it's fine to pick a typeface out of the can as a starting point, no typeface can ever anticipate the idiosyncrasies of the name [brand] that you are creating, nor can it perfectly match the design principles of the icon or supporting graphics."

Matthew Clark, Subplot Design

informant

informant

informant

informant

informant

informant

informant

informant

informant

informant

informant

informant

Brief 03

●●●

Namestyle & symbol

The brief

Design a distinctive and meaningful namestyle and symbol for a donor card

The brief explained

Target market

The target market for Donorcard is over-18s with a social conscience. Donorcard is also aimed at enticing new, possibly younger donors to the register. There is no specific socio-economic band. The main aim of the Donorcard campaign is that cardholders feel good about their ultimate generosity.

Requirements

The namestyle may be "Donorcard" or a name of your choice, which may be one word or a group of words. The namestyle should be accompanied by, or include, an appropriately representative symbol. The namestyle must interpret your chosen name typographically, so as to create a distinctive and meaningful image that includes a symbol. The design is to be used not only on the cards that people carry with them, but also on other informational and promotional material, so the namestyle must be able to function both in color and black-and-white, as well as at both comparatively small and large scales. It is important that the word "Donorcard," or its substitute, be visually interesting and clear to read: the design should encourage younger people to carry the card, and must also make the card instantly recognizable.

01 Client: Love
Design: Grundini

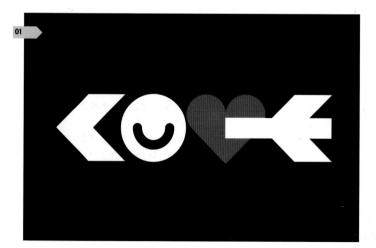

ProfessionalCare

02 Client: Professional Care
Design: Grundini

Wolverhampton
Domestic Violence Forum

03/04/05 Client: Wolverhampton Domestic
Violence Forum
Design: Bright Pink

---

05 ▶

If you wish to leave, then these organisations
can advise you. There are places you can go
and live safely

The Haven
01902
Support for women
suffering domestic violence
713001
24 hours a day
www.havenrefuge.org.uk

The items on this list are not
essential, but if you are planning
to leave you may consider taking:

Benefit books
Money
Bank books & cards
Driving licence
Family Photographs
Birth certificates
Change of clothes
Passports/Visas
Keys
Childs favourite toy
Medicines

Housing &
Social Services
01902
556556
Mon-Fri 9-5pm

The National
Domestic Violence
Helpline
01902
552999
out of hrs

0808
2000247
24hrs

In an emergency dial 999

If you are being abused you
may feel alone and unable
to make any real decisions

Advice & Support ?

The organisations listed on
this card will offer advice
and support that may help

Methodology

Research

Study existing namestyles and symbols and, in
particular, designs that have been created for similar
target markets and associated circumstances. The
context for this namestyle is comparatively complex–
it must speak to all ages, but especially to younger
people. It should inspire them to carry the card as
"the thing" to do, yet also give them an understanding
of the serious nature of the proposition. Referencing
a wide range of namestyles and symbols will be
useful, but focus on examples that embrace design
decisions suitable for a donor card.

Exploration and thumbnails

Experiment with different names for the donor card
and make your selection. Your namestyle should be
based on a regular font that embodies the character
required for the card. Ask yourself, should the
typeface be serif or sans serif; rounded or angular;
italic, bold, light, or medium? Think carefully about
the implications of each and its ultimate impact upon
legibility and the character of the final design. At the
same time, you must give careful consideration to
the creation of the symbol. This can be accommodated
in two ways. The first option is to use the symbol
as a substitute for, or augmentation to, one of the
letterforms that make up the namestyle. The second
is to create a separate symbol that is related to the
type through alignment and visual association.
If you substitute an appropriate shape or icon for

one or more letters, check that the namestyle
remains legible. Given the subject matter of this
project, there are a number of obvious iconic images:
a heart (a simplistic interpretation or a medical
version), an eye, kidneys and other organs, or hands
in a benevolent gesture. At this stage it is important
to think about color. Red, perhaps the most obvious
choice, could also be the most successful, as it can
have a deep tone that offers a great number of
options for tints. Blue and green, both suggestive
of caring, also have medical associations.

When producing thumbnails for your namestyle,
use different weights and colors of pen or pencil on
marker paper. Work with a minimum of two large
sheets of marker paper, tracing through elements
from one sheet to the other. You will often find that
while part of a design is satisfactory, other sections
require amending; if you can trace the good elements
in this way, you need redraw only those details that
need changing. This will save you much time and
possible heartache. Explore alternative typefaces
and weights, expanded and condensed letterforms,

upper- and lowercase letters, colors, and spatial relationships between letters, words, and symbols. Try out as many alternative ideas as possible, then stand back and assess the design options. View them at different sizes and in monochrome as well as color. It is always a very good idea to get opinions from a number of other people; ask them to interpret the designs before giving them the precise details of the brief.

After choosing one or possibly two of the most successful concepts, progress these designs by making many different small adjustments: bring the letters closer together or move them farther apart, enlarge or reduce the size or weight of certain letters, consider different shades or hues of a particular element, add an icon or substitute shape in another way. Continue working in this way until the namestyle and accompanying symbol are really beginning to express the desired character.

Design development

You could now start developing your design solutions on-screen. Well-considered visual assessment of the detail in thumbnail designs is vital; take careful note of the weight of letterforms, their proportional relationships and spacing, and whether your letter-forms are in any way condensed or expanded. A useful technique at this stage is to scan your selected thumbnail designs and use the digital files to guide you in creating the final computer-generated solutions. As you develop the finished visual, print out the namestyle and symbol at a variety of scales so that you make the right judgments for print and for screen. This process is vital, as printed versions can appear very different from their on-screen counterparts, even to the most experienced designer.

Don't be afraid to work on both hand-generated thumbnails and computerized versions—the interplay of media can be very helpful.

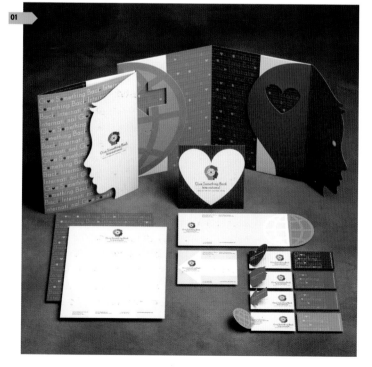

01

02

Give Something Back
International

01/02 Client: Give Something Back
Design: Gee + Chung Design

04

03/04 Client: b:RAP
Design: boing!

Completion

Having produced a final namestyle and symbol, apply the design to a credit card-sized card. Think about supporting information that will also need to appear on this card, making sure your design decisions "belong" to the styles and formats within the namestyle and symbol. The positioning of elements within the card design must echo any relationships and alignments you have already set up.

Your solutions for the namestyle and symbol are best displayed on a neutral background, in color and black-and-white, and at different sizes. These designs should be accompanied by the finished donor card, which will help to demonstrate the application of the identity in context. Both print and online presentations are practical ways to display your design solutions; digital files of your designs can be uploaded to personal or commercial portfolio sites.

The examples on this spread are for similar organizations, but were selected for two very different reasons. The one showing the church depicted as a drill is humorous and applied dramatically to great effect. The second provides a fascinating insight into the design process. Both show how important it is to consider the relationship between type and symbol.

01

02

ST. MARY'S CHURCH RESTORATION FUND

Frank Padginton
Building Site Manager

St. Marychurch Street
Rotherhithe
London SE16 4JET
Tel. 020 7231 2465

01/02/03/04 Client: St Mary's Church, Rotherhithe

Design: Rose Design

03

Caution
Wet Paint

Thou Shalt Not Touch.

04

Caution
Wet Paint

Thou Shalt Not Touch.

ST. MARY'S CHURCH RESTORATION FUND

05

06

05/06/07/08 Client: Historic St George's
United Methodist Church

Design: Paone Design

07

08

Although these examples are all quite disparate, they are all relevant to the Donorcard brief.

01

02

03

01 Client: The Swedish Writers' Union
Design: BankerWessel

02 Client: LifeCatching
Design: Sayles Graphic Design

03 Client: Brahma Kumaris
Design: Sonsoles Llorens

04

05

06

07

six·o·eight

04 Client: International Policy Network, London
Design: With Relish

05 Client: Living Raw
Design: Sayles Graphic Design

06 Client: Red Cross
Design: BankerWessel

07 Client: Six.o.Eight Fine Jewelry
Design: Edmund Li

Solutions

Project: Namestyle and symbol
Design: Bright Pink

These visuals look at configurations of typefaces, upper- and lowercase letterforms, color relationships, and simple iconic symbols for the donor card project. Arrows represent the donation of organs; brackets reflect the saving and protecting of an organ so it can be given to someone else, and the star implies the promise of a bright future.

donorcard

DONORCARD

Donorcard

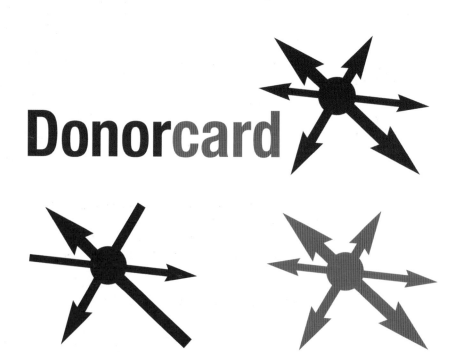

{DONOR}
CARD

If I die, please give any of
my functioning organs to help
someone else.

signature

_____

Donorcard

If I die, please give any of
my functioning organs to help
someone else.

signature _____

DONOR
CARD

If I die, please give any of
my functioning organs to help
someone else.

signature

_____

{donor}card

{DONOR}CARD

{DONOR}CARD

"By giving a tint to backgrounds, type or symbols can be set
either on top in a darker color, or reversed through in white
or a paler tint. This opens up numerous possibilities and
can create surprisingly pleasing designs with interesting
contrasts of scale."

Carolyn Knight and Jessica Glaser, Bright Pink

Project: Namestyle and symbol
Design: Bright Pink

These concepts use the name "it's a gift" for the
donor card and the symbol is a simple interpretation
of this—a parcel wrapped with flowing ribbons.
Of the typefaces tested, the solid sans serif italic relates
best to the mark-making of the symbol and also has
a friendliness, yet professionalism, which is appropriate
for the subject. The parcel image is used as a border
pattern and reversed white through the background,
to provide a dynamic contrast in scale.

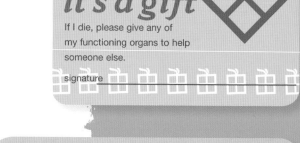

Project: Namestyle and symbol
Design: Bright Pink

In these concepts, the first "o" in donorcard has
been replaced with a heart. The stylized nature
of the heart allows it to represent organs generally
rather than the heart alone, and also to give a sense
of the continued life and love that organ donation
makes possible. The vibrant pink is highly visible,
but potential associations with femininity could
be off-putting to male participants in this scheme.

"The role of the typeface is either to 'get out of the way,' or to be sympathetic
to the values of an identity, so where an icon communicates most of
the brand concept, the typeface may help to promote softer values like
'approachable,' 'casual,' or 'progressive.'"

Matthew Clark, Subplot Design

Brief 04

●●●

Linked identities

The brief

Design linked, enduring namestyles for three companies that are part of The Energyflo Group

The brief explained

Target market

The target market for Energyflo companies is domestic energy consumers with a regard for the environment. The Energyflo customer prioritizes the environmental impact of domestic utilities over the cost of supplies. The high profile of environmental issues will make consumers feel good about choosing Energyflo companies.

01/02 Client: Via Motif
Design: Vrontikis Design Office

Requirements

To design namestyles for the following companies:

- Ecolectric from Energyflo
- Gaspower from Energyflo
- Watermetering from Energyflo

Energyflo is a holding company for different energy providers. Each of these three companies requires an individual identity that also relates to the style and image of The Energyflo Group as a whole.

All three companies have a high regard for the environment. Ecolectric generates electricity by wave and wind power, and also through recovering energy from waste management. Although gas is a nonrenewable resource and cannot be classed as a green energy, Gaspower from Energyflo gives customers the option of offsetting greenhouse gas emissions by financing projects that help to reduce global warming. Watermetering from Energyflo promotes the responsible use of water, providing customers with efficient metering and consumption-control systems.

Each namestyle can use up to three colors, but must also function in a single-color application in the contexts of both print and screen. Designs must be applied to a range of stationery, vehicles, printed literature, web pages and eco-product packaging. You must also produce a branding palette to demonstrate the scope and flexibility of design solutions.

01

02

Methodology

Research

There are many companies that own and promote
a variety of brands in a similar way to the Energyflo
group described in this brief. Take time to assess
how these associations function and also to
understand how the values of a company can be
communicated by each of the individual brands in
its portfolio. It is worth analyzing the commonalities
and differences in values that these brands present
to the consumer in order get a clear understanding
of how their affiliations and hierarchies operate.
Be sure to look into both the visual and the verbal
tone of voice adopted by the companies you research.
An organization could advocate its concern for a
cause in a number of ways, using well-written text,
a carefully selected color scheme, thoughtful and
relevant use of imagery, or a mix of all three.

    Take particular note of the associations
in the visual and verbal language used to identify
the brand. What are the common themes and
connections that appear in the promotion of
the brand, and how are these themes extended
throughout the breadth of design requirements?

Exploration and thumbnails

Once you have spent some time researching complex
brand structures and their applications, it is time
to begin designing and exploring alternatives. One
of the keys to successfully designing, developing,
and implementing a complex brand identity is to
ensure that, from the outset, design ideas have
scope for development while also possessing clear
visual connections and associations. A good way to
begin is to write out the brand and company names,
then carefully analyze the forms, structures, and
counterforms of the letters. Look for commonalities,
differences, unusual shapes and marks, and
repetition. Think about whether a symbol would
benefit the brand identity and experiment with
various alternatives. Try out different relationships of
scale and positioning to find what best communicates
the essence and activity of The Energyflo Group.
Remember, no design decision is ever made in
isolation—every choice is made in relation to another
and will impact upon future design options and
possibilities. The namestyles in this branding brief
represent just the beginning of your task: it is their

application in both 2D and 3D form and for use on-screen that will demonstrate whether your identity can function effectively.

While working on your rough designs, think about the use of color. Again, try to establish themes that will help reinforce the connection between the three Energyflo brands. An excellent way of extending the scope of an identity palette is to play with the primary and secondary color palette, changing which is which from company to company. This can refresh the overall brand and provide a pleasing design surprise that, in turn, influences an audience's perception of a brand. While exploring color, investigate the use of imagery. Work through alternatives of scale, cropping, grouping, and positioning. Be sure that any imagery you use looks as though it belongs together and has been art-directed to follow and promote the same themes.

Textures and patterns can prove a useful addition to a branding palette. As with any element that forms part of a brand identity, a texture or pattern should have a distinct visual connection with the other design characteristics of the brand.

No doubt you will need to use a mix of hand- and computer-generated design details to help you establish pleasing and appropriate visual relationships. Use your thumbnail designs to decide which typographic details "fit" the style and character of Energyflo and its three sub-brands. Make sure you take the possible hierarchical complexities of this project into account; these will demand a variety of textural and tonal detailing.

Design development

After working through rough visuals for the 2D and 3D requirements of this brief, take time to stand back and assess which design options have the most potential. Canvass opinion from colleagues and other designers, as this discussion process is an excellent way to stimulate design development and is also likely to highlight issues and consequences you haven't foreseen. Assess the designs for each of the Energyflo companies not only in relationship to the other two, but also next to the identities of actual utility providers. Having established which are the most successful solutions, refine your designs, remembering to view print-based solutions as printouts and not just on-screen. Before finalizing your designs, double-check them for consistency across the many elements of this brief: check color consistency, as changes of media can have a noticeable effect on color appearance; and check typographic detail, including consistency of face, scale, leading, tracking, weight, spacing, orientation, and positioning.

01/02 Client: Barcelona Energy Agency
Design: Sonsoles Llorens

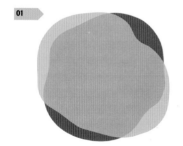

AGÈNCIA D'ENERGIA
DE BARCELONA

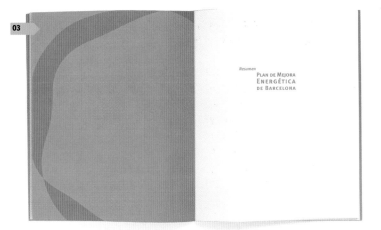

04

Completion

A broad branding palette will make an impressive and comprehensive display in a portfolio. Show the breadth of your Energyflo design and be sure to display a range of 2D and 3D applications that not only demonstrate the scope of your designs, but also illustrate the shared brand values of and visual connections between Ecolectric, Gaspower, and Watermetering. Both print and online presentations are practical ways to display your design solutions; digital files of your designs can be uploaded to personal or commercial portfolio sites.

Both of these examples show how varied an application should be in order to communicate the diverse and complex messages associated with a brand.

01/02/03/04 Client: ACR Heat Products
Design: twelve20

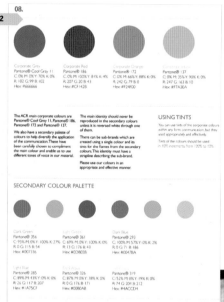

SECONDARY COLOUR PALETTE

OUR COLOURS

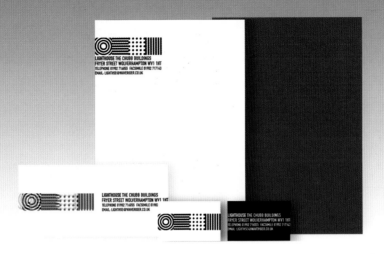

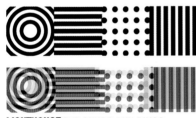

05 Client: Lighthouse Media Centre

Design: boing!

All of these thumbnails and solutions relate to the topic of energy and provide a wealth of material for inspiration. The various alternatives show the subtle changes and developments that are essential for thorough exploration of ideas and the satisfactory resolution of design challenges.

01/02/03
Client: National Semiconductor Corporation
Design: Gee + Chung Design

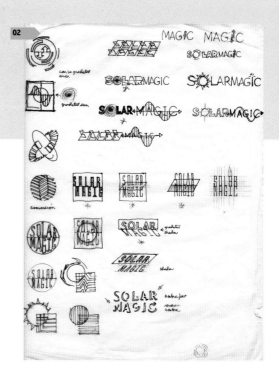

04/05/06 Client: National
Semiconductor Corporation
Design: Gee + Chung Design

Solutions

Project: Linked identities

Design: Amy-Claire Morgan

Simple shapes and distinct colors characterize these designs for the three companies that make up the Energyflo group. The appealing, modern color palette avoids the cliché of existing visual codes and is used to great effect with gray to create brand continuity throughout. The concept involves changing the priorities of symbols and namestyles, with the symbols being used dramatically in isolation at a number of different scales.

"At the start of any identity project, it is essential for the designer to avoid any preconceptions of a client category and to keep an open mind by conducting a thorough visual audit of the brands that exist within the client's specific industry. The purpose is to learn what symbols, styles, and colors are commonly used within the client's industry, and what is appropriate for the client's audience."

Earl Gee, Gee + Chung Design

Project: Linked identities
Design: Anette Mosdøl

Anette Mosdøl's design offers a very different solution from Amy-Claire Morgan's. She has interpreted the three subsidiary companies as part of a whole and uses quarters of a circle to develop this theme. The rounded corners of picture boxes and repetitive use of circular shapes keep this theme consistent throughout the design. Muted, dusky colors make up an unusual color palette and the use of graduated tints adds interest. Even the lightweight, rounded letterforms of the typeface connect with this shape. One issue worth considering, however, is that lightweight sans serif letterforms tend to fill in when used at small scale, and this will reduce their legibility.

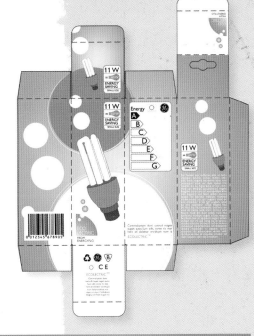

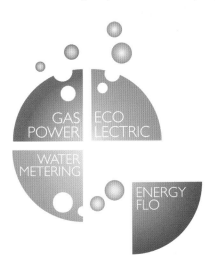

Project: Linked identities
Design: Grace Oakley

Dynamic simplicity is key in this design, with the strong, single letterforms having mnemonic impact throughout all applications. The designs are flexible, as the bold "E," "G," and "W" can be used at different scales and without supporting type. The illustrative shapes cut into each letterform indicate the utility marketed by that brand. Given the complexity of the brand structure, it is possibly rather limiting to allocate only one color to each section of Energflo, as the scope required includes supporting information that will be difficult to communicate without at least one other option.

Project: Linked identities
Design: Matthew Preston

Matthew Preston has selected animals that embody the nature of the Energyflo brands as symbols for the individual companies. This is an effective way of highlighting the environmental ethos of the companies and an extremely persuasive means of attracting custom. Simple silhouettes allow a flexible application, including the use of cutouts and of both positive and negative images. The lowercase sans serif type adds to the impact of the highly visible color palette.

"An unusual color choice for a particular industry can help the company stand out from its competition and connect with its audience, as long as the color selected supports the brand strategy and avoids any negative international or cultural symbology."

Earl Gee, Gee + Chung Design

Brief 05

●●●

Branding palette

The brief

Establish a broad branding palette for the Coleman Institute

The brief explained

Target market

The target market is two-fold: prospective students looking for a high standard of education, and companies and organizations interested in business development and commissioning cutting-edge research. Coleman Institute is a high-caliber university and fees are pitched accordingly; the target market values education and research over savings.

01/02 Client: Business to Arts
Design: Brighten the Corners

Requirements

The Coleman Institute is a San Francisco-based university with a reputation for high-quality research and teaching in areas including science, technology, ecology, and environmentalism.

The branding palette must include a namestyle and a strapline. The identity should reflect the Coleman Institute's areas of expertise and, to a certain degree, its geographic location. The palette should include recommendations for use of color, typographic styling, use and style of imagery, grouping of elements, a decorative textural design, and notes on tone of voice. These elements should be applied to a varied range of 2D and 3D design contexts, and should demonstrate the scope and flexibility of the identity effectively. Areas of application should include design for print and design for screen. The identity should function effectively in both color and black-and-white.

01 ▶
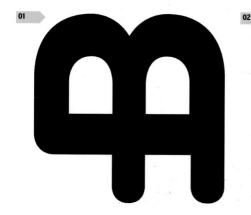

02 ▶

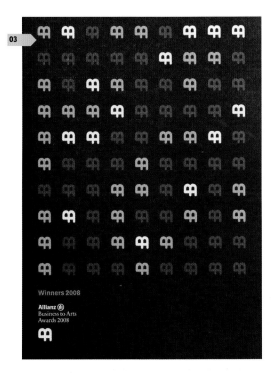

Winners 2008

Allianz ⑪
Business to Arts
Awards 2008

⑪

Methodology

Research

Large organizations require complex visual identities. A branding palette outlines the design approach of the brand and explains, simply and clearly, how all the various design elements—typestyles, colors, shapes, patterns—can be combined and applied in different contexts.

To undertake the research necessary for this project, it is important to have a visual overview of a broad range of branded items, from both 2D and 3D contexts, and produced by a variety of educational organizations, such as universities and colleges. Many of these educational institutes will have specialist areas, or will teach subjects for which they are particularly renowned; assess how this expertise and these reputations have been communicated. Analyze the use of type styles and typographic relationships; look for combinations of typographic detail that are used repeatedly in designs produced by an organization. Take particular note of the use of color within a range of branded elements: have there

been any shifts in priority or tone of color, and how is color being positioned and used as a branding element? Examine the employment and function of imagery. Is there a recurring style of photography or illustration, and how are images grouped, positioned, or cropped? Study detail including the use of rules, dotted and dashed lines, and, most importantly, look at spacing. Is there a consistent amount of space between or around individual elements, and how is space used between paragraphs and headings? Have the designers of the brands you researched originated any textures or repeat patterns as part of their design, and, if so, how are these components used? Are there any distinctive materials common to these brands? If there are, analyze their significance—what do these substances bring to the design? Are there any common design elements, such as the use of a specific angle, curve, or shape? Look also for visual links and associations that make connections between the diverse elements and ingredients that comprise the brand.

The answers to all of these questions will help you build up a comprehensive image of the influences and elements that come together in the creation of a branding palette. Record your visual responses to these questions on palette sheets, and group elements in a manner sympathetic to the individual design systems you assess.

03/04 Client: Business to Arts
Design: Brighten the Corners

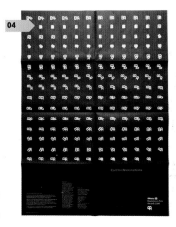

Exploration and thumbnails

Having researched influential and inspiring design examples and built up a good understanding of what is meant by a comprehensive branding palette, it is time to begin exploring design options for Coleman Institute. A good way to begin is to letter out the name "Coleman Institute." Observe the structure of letterforms and work through different typefaces to find which best communicates the character, appeal, and expertise of the organization. Look at symbols you could use in association with the typographic namestyle to reinforce the meaning of the brand. Consider the possible benefits of using a strapline and how this might help explain the values of Coleman Institute.

Sometimes looking at typographic detail will inspire a visual theme. For example, a circular letterform might suggest the use of rounded shapes, or rounded corners for image boxes. Visual associations are an important part of a branding palette. Having established links, look into the scope and impact they are likely to have on other areas of the brand, including use of imagery, format, materials, structures, folding systems, patterns, and textures. Decide how best to develop considered associations in order to bring cohesion, consistency, and variety to the design.

01

02

03

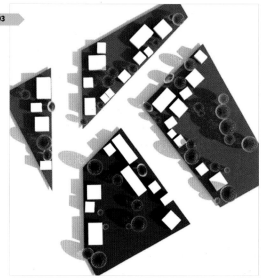

01/02/03 Client: Kutina town
Design: Studio International

Design development

Progress through a variety of different options and see what other designers and colleagues feel are the most successful solutions, and why. Start to bring actual type and image together, work through a number of realistic combinations that represent the potential design approaches necessary for the implementation of Coleman Institute's brand.

Demonstrate the design scope of the brand by selecting a number of items to visualize. Ideally this selection should include both print- and screen-based designs, as well as items from a 3D context.

Completion

Coleman Institute's branding palette is a complicated project to present, as final designs are likely to involve a multitude of elements and a mix of media and dimensions. Use palette sheets similar to those compiled during your research for this project. They will form an integral aspect of your presentation as they illustrate, without the need for explanatory text, how to use Coleman Institute branding. Screenshots are a helpful way of displaying a screen-based application within a print portfolio, and a selection of photographs is likely to be the simplest way of showcasing 3D visuals. Examples of the brand functioning within an editorial context can be shown mounted as double-page spreads, or made up as multipage visuals. Online presentation can also be a very practical way to display your design solutions; whether as a PDF or as separate digital images, designs can be uploaded to personal or commercial portfolio sites.

04 Client: Texas Children's Hospital
Design: Design by Principle

Color is a significant element in these examples. Both involve a broad palette that provides scope to embrace all aspects of the identity. Typefaces, style of illustration, and graphic patterns all have an integral part to play in the execution of the branding.

01

---

01 Client: Dealerward

Design: Studio8 Design and Applied Works

02 Client: Brand Tailor

Design: ArthurSteenHorneAdamson

02

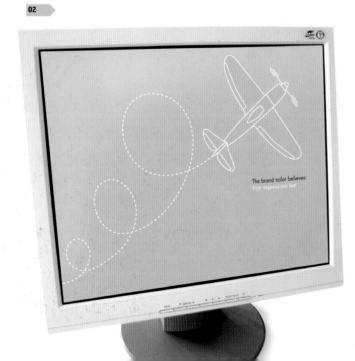

An identity for an educational institution needs to impart a complex range of messages: that the institution runs a professional business, is a successful educator, and has an appealing environment, to name but a few. The identities shown here achieve all of these goals, establishing audience recognition and loyalty.

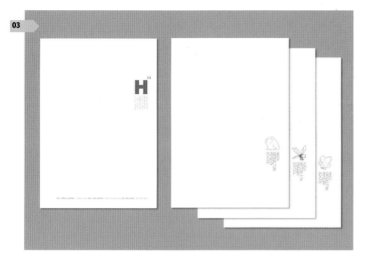

03 Client: Hugh Myddelton Primary School
Design: ArthurSteenHorneAdamson

04 Client: Vancouver Aquarium
Design: Subplot Design

In both of these examples, distinctive color and typographic styling are used to create strong identities: "bridge" is a good example of an appropriate visual metaphor; the pages from the University of Pennsylvania prospectus use pattern and composition to provide discrete layouts.

01/02/03 Client: Belron International
Design: Rose Design

22.09.04

To help you get used to all our new programs and systems, we'll be providing training in every aspect of the business.

From 22 September we will be holding workshops, group, and one-to-one sessions to take you through your paces.

The courses consist of up to ten stages. Once you have completed all stages, you'll be able to use every new system.

DEPARTMENT OF FINE ARTS
MASTER OF FINE ARTS PROGRAM

20
04
05.

PennDesign

THE SCHOOL OF DESIGN
OF THE UNIVERSITY OF PENNSYLVANIA

PAINTING
PRINTMAKING
SCULPTURE
PHOTOGRAPHY
NEW MEDIA

MFA PROGRAM

MFA Courses
- Studio Concentration: Painting, Printmaking, Sculpture,
  Photography, Combined Media
- Collage/Montage
- Computer Seminar: Digital Imaging
- Critical Issues Seminar
- Drawing Seminar
- Graduate Sculpture Seminar
- Graduate Photography Seminar
- Intersections: Meaning & Making in Public Art
- Significant Matters: Form Language in the Visual Arts

MFA Faculty
Terry Adkins, Laurie Churchman, Susana Jacobson, John Moore, Joshua Mosley, Hitoshi Nakazato, Julie Spencer Schneider, Jackie Tileston. In addition 2005-2006 senior critics Alfred Leslie, Paolo Osuna, Nigel Rolfe, Judith Stein, Robert Storr and Alan Worth.

MFA Studios
Graduate studios are located in the Morgan Building, Furness Fine Arts Building, and Franklin Annex. The Morgan Building, c. 1920, renovated in 1990, houses 45 studios averaging 250 square feet. Designed by architects Cope and Stewardson, the arts and crafts style building features central gallery and meeting areas, surrounded by studios with natural light. Printmaking studios for silk screen, lithography, relief, monoprint, etching, drypoint, and photo-print processes, as well as administrative offices are located in Morgan.

Additional photographs and painting studios are located in the Duhring Wing of the Furness Fine Arts Building, which also houses the Fisher Fine Arts Library and the Arthur Ross Gallery. Photography darkrooms are located in Charles Addams Fine Arts Hall. All sculpture candidates are provided with Penn Design studios in Franklin Annex. Technical resources include large, well-equipped shops with facilities for wood, clay, plaster, and metal fabrication, as well as associate computer labs. MFAs are allowed 24-hour, 7-day a week access to fine arts facilities.

MFA RESOURCES

Architectural Archives
The Architectural Archives of the University of Pennsylvania preserves the works of more than 200 designers from the 18th century to the present.

Arthur Ross Gallery
The gallery presents a year-round schedule of art exhibitions, including objects from the University's collections, and other major public and private collections. The Gallery also offers public lectures and tours, children's programs, and traveling exhibitions with an interdisciplinary appeal and international focus.

Fisher Fine Arts Library
The collections of the Fisher Fine Arts Library include over 125,000 volumes and 900 current serial subscriptions. In addition, the Library also houses the Perkins Library, a collection of more than 3,000 rare architectural titles. The Library also houses the Slide Collection, a teaching collection of 495,000 slides, 60,000 photographs, and 45,000 digital images.

Department of The History of Art
The graduate department offers courses leading to the A.M. and Ph.D. degrees in the history of art, concentrating on the art of the Western world from the ancient period to the twentieth century. Programs in Asian, Eastern, Islamic, and South Asian art are also offered.

Kelly Writers House
Founded in 1995, the Kelly Writers House is a hub of creative writing on campus where distinguished authors like John Updike, Robert Creeley, Tony Kushner, and Grace Paley meet with Penn writers, poets, and filmmakers. The School of Design and Kelly Writers House present the Poet Painter Series among the many programs and projects that promote the rich range of contemporary literature, addressing writing both as a practice and as an object of study.

Solutions

Project: Branding palette
Design: Paul Power

The Coleman Institute brand has to be flexible enough to allow its successful application in a broad range of promotional and educational contexts. The cellular structure of the symbol not only reflects the multifaceted expertise of the institution, but also relates to its scientific and technological focus, while providing scope for varied use. The visuals demonstrate some of the 2D and 3D situations in which this identity would be used.

Always double-check spelling and punctuation, even in your roughs and visuals. The wrong number of characters in a word or, as in this case, the omission of an apostrophe—before the "s" in "Nature's Answer"—changes the length of the line and also the shape of the word. Not only can this can have a knock-on effect, it can also suggest a lack of attention to detail.

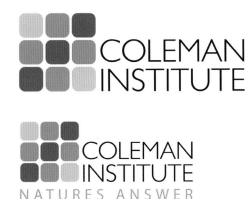

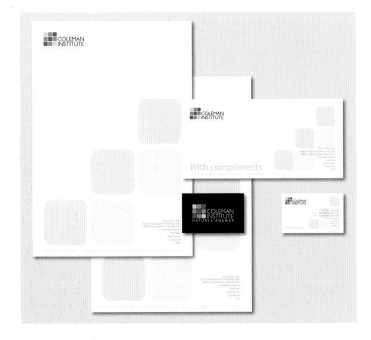

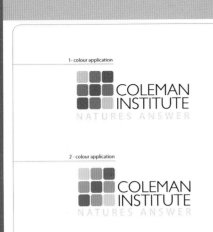

1- colour application

2 - colour application

Our brand colours (On a white background)

When the Coleman Institute brand marks are used on a white background, only the following colour versions may be applied.

2 - colour application
This is the preferred brand mark versoion used for all print and screen based media.

1 - colour application
Where ever one colour is availible you must stick to this guidlines in order to come up with the best solution. In black and white the logo should still read well like i have shown.

In case where a third-party colour is availible, please ensure to consult with Marketing Department in the first instance.

Coleman Institute Brand Guidelines
Issue 1 December 2008
©Coleman Institute Limited

"Typeface selection within the context of identity development is critically important. It is quite possible to choose a font that, due to its inherent formal qualities, aids in the communication of its subject. Careful evaluation should also be given to the typeface's legibility, especially when used at small sizes and in media which may compromise its readability due to production or resolution limitations."

Gregory Paone, Paone Design Associates

Project: Branding palette
Design: Ingrid Velure

Ingrid Velure's identity is an excellent example of the scope of a successful branding palette. She has incorporated a range of linked colors, textures, shapes, typographic systems, and compositional relationships that are distinctively applied in a great range of contexts. For the Coleman Institute mark she has adopted a symbol that makes direct visual reference to the opening pages of a book, and the jagged edges of this book are used to create shaped picture boxes and divisional elements in printed material. Ingrid's branding palette includes the strapline "Brighten your future!" which she has interpreted in a complementary handwritten, informal style.

Brighten your future!

"The breadth and variety of visual elements available within a concept ensure that both flexibility and continuity can be achieved."

Carolyn Knight and Jessica Glaser, Bright Pink

COLEMAN institute · science

Facts

Brighten your future!

COLEMAN institute · technology

COLEMAN institute

Pantone 288 C	Pantone Process Cyan C	Pantone 297 C	Pantone 375 C	Pantone 373 C	Pantone 266 C	Pantone 264 C

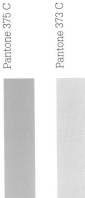

Photography *Jeffrey Graetsch*

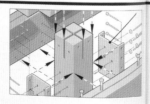

Section 03
Page layout

Page layout is one of the most important graphic design disciplines. Its fundamental aspect—namely the careful control of visual hierarchy—has a strong bearing on every other area of graphic design.

If you would like to improve or simply extend your page layout skills, then you will find a helpful, challenging, and inspiring brief to suit your needs here.

Designs that extend across multiple pages, whether in books, magazines, brochures, or newspapers, are referred to as page layout or editorial designs. As readers of the printed page we all have experience of the reassurance and comfort that comes from holding paper pages in our hands, knowing we will have those pages for as long as we choose to keep a publication. Is this also true of websites and blogs, or is the experience of looking at a screen a completely different one? Many well-respected designers and writers believe it is different. Lee Carter, editor-in-chief of online fashion magazine *Hint*, says, "Websites can't offer the tactile experience that glossies can, but glossies can't compete with the enhancing effects of light from a screen." Patrick Burgoyne of *Creative Review* says of screen-based magazines, "The challenge for designers is to take these opportunities [presented by the diverse forms of online publishing] and use them to create products that are as useful and compelling to readers as those of their print antecedents."

01 Client: Royal Academy of Arts
Design: Studio8 Design

01

02

02 Client: Christian Education

Design: twelve20

The printed page allows for more typographic and compositional design variety than the screen. Designers working on screen-based pages often have to weigh up the balance of accessibility versus aesthetics. However, the print designer does not have the option of using movement, sound, or speedy links to other relevant sources of information.

Confronted with a page layout project, one of the first tasks of the graphic designer is to read the text in detail to get a good understanding of what is being discussed. The designer as reader, taking on the role of the target audience, must interpret the intended hierarchy and possibly augment it or suggest hierarchical alternatives that will improve audience understanding of and participation with the design. Hierarchical control is the effective sequencing of the separate visual elements that make up each design, giving the reader easy access to information in an order that is carefully and skillfully controlled. This degree of design-led control can result in some surprising designs. Encouraging readers to engage with editorial design is a vital role for the graphic designer. The topic of a design may not be of particular interest to an audience, but as a professional editorial designer, it is your job not only to attract attention, but also to hold interest. It is important to guarantee that information is accessed in the manner and order that you intend and, ideally, to ensure that an audience enjoys the experience of interacting with your design. The reader needs to be tempted by "digestible" amounts of information

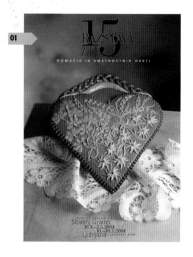

01

01/02 Zbornica Slovenije

Design: Krog

that are presented in a recognizable order. Many examples of contemporary page layout have to communicate a great deal of complex information; hierarchies are not created simply to provide visual interest, but to ensure that the intended audience can take on board as much information as possible. The visual hierarchy and organization of a design can be controlled using a combination of imagery, typographic texture and tone, strong groupings, a flexible grid structure, and changes of scale. All of these elements come together under the careful guidance of the designer who forms the overall visual aesthetic of a project.

Grids play a useful role in almost every graphic design genre, but in the discipline of page layout, a grid structure is a vital organizational tool. Rob Carter, Ben Day, and Philip Meggs describe a grid as "a valuable framework for structuring typographic and pictorial elements. The grid produces a cohesiveness that can improve legibility and the communication of ideas." When asked about his approach to the use of grids, Jeff Leak of boing! says, "I always try to use a grid based on an odd number of columns as this creates asymmetry which I think is more intriguing to the reader and often forces me to make more dynamic use of space." Jeff continues, "I always try to design grids in a way that allows for a lot of design flexibility. For example, I would be very unlikely to settle for a two- or three-column grid; I would be much more likely to consider using a structure divided into eight or nine columns, as this would provide much more scope."

02

There is obviously room for various interpretations and approaches to page layout. Some of the many consistent factors and considerations are covered in the following briefs. Whether designing a printed brochure or an online magazine, attention to the detailing of hierarchies, visual texture and tone, and composition will influence audience enthusiasm. Although the three briefs refer specifically to print-based design, if screen-based editorial design holds a special fascination for you, the first two briefs can be easily adapted. The third brief, designing an arts program, could also suit a screen-based delivery, but it requires a carefully considered conceptual development in order to realize the project's full potential.

03 Client: *Plastique Magazine*

Design: Studio8 Design

Glossary

alignment the arrangement of image and text in a design, typically from a left, right, central, top, or bottom axis

art direction management of the creative and production process for a given project, including instructing a photographer or illustrator on the content and composition of an image

binding the manner in which the cover is attached and the pages are collated for a printed publication

bleed when a page or cover design extends to and off the edge of the paper it is called a "bleed"

body copy/body type the main text excluding headlines and subheads; in visuals this can be nonsensical

condensed letterforms letters in which the set widths of the characters are narrower than in a standard typeface

dummy a mock-up with designed pages as well as blank pages to imitate the "feel" of the final publication

elements of design the building blocks of design: color, shape, size, space, line, value, and texture

expanded letterforms letters in which the set widths of the characters are wider than in a standard typeface

format the size, proportions, and orientation (landscape or portrait) of a printed piece

four-color process/full-color process the printing process that reproduces colors by combining cyan, magenta, yellow, and black

genre an artistic type or style; an area of expertise

grids the invisible lines imposed on a layout that help to bring coordination by providing guides for alignment and scale

gutter the space between columns of text

hierarchy (visual hierarchy) the arrangement of elements to guide viewers through them in a specific order

landscape a page or layout that is wider than it is tall

leading the space between lines of type

margin space without type at the edges of pages, including between pages at the spine

marker paper specialist flimsy paper with a coating that prevents marker pens from bleeding through to surfaces below

masthead the credit box on the front of a publication, headed by the publication name and listing selected information such as publishers, editors, writers, and others, along with the publication's office address, subscription details, etc.

mnemonic assisting or intending to assist memory

paper stock a particular kind and weight of paper; the paper to be printed on

portrait a page or layout that is taller than it is wide

sans serif a style of typeface without serifs, i.e., without ornamental strokes on the ends of characters. Common sans serif typefaces include Arial, Helvetica, AvantGarde, and Verdana

spread/double-page spread (DPS) two pages that appear together when a book or publication is opened, i.e. two facing pages

system (design system) the set of criteria used to organize the various elements of design in relation to each other to form a considered whole

thumbnails comparatively small rough visuals that incorporate sufficient detail and accuracy to be of value for decision-making

tracking the letterspacing applied across a line of text

typographic case uppercase or lowercase

typographic weight the thickness or thinness of letterforms, creating different degrees of bold, medium, or light type

x-height the height of the lowercase letters, excluding ascenders and descenders

Reading list

Basics Design: Layout
Gavin Ambrose and Paul Harris

Best of Brochure Design 9
Jason Godfrey

**Book-Art: Innovation in
Book Design**
Charlotte Rivers

Graphis Brochures 6
Martin Pedersen

Great British Editorial
Emeyele

**Grid Systems: Principles
of Organizing Type**
Kimberly Elam

Issues: New Magazine Design
Jeremy Leslie

**Mag-Art: Innovation in
Magazine Design**
Charlotte Rivers

Magazine Design That Works
Stacey King

**magCulture: New
Magazine Design**
Jeremy Leslie

**Making and Breaking the
Grid: A Layout Design
Workshop**
Timothy Samara

Pages/Editorial Design
Màrius Sala

**Stop Stealing Sheep and
Find Out How Type Works**
Erik Spiekermann and E. M. Ginger

Type & Typography
Phil Baines and Andrew Haslam

Equipment

- Scalpel
- Marker paper
- Pencils
- Markers/colored pencils
- Steel ruler
- Set square
- Stapler
- Typeface reference
- Cutting mat
- Spray adhesive
- Lightweight card
- Professional color-matching reference
- Computer/software

Brief 01

● ○ ○

Magazine cover & spreads

The brief

Design a front cover and two double-page spreads for a new magazine called *Arkitekt*

The brief explained

Target market

The target market is both male and female readers with an interest in architecture and architectural design. *Arkitekt* is a high-end magazine aimed at students, professionals, and amateurs who value an informed awareness and knowledge of international contemporary design.

Requirements

The format of the magazine is up to you. The double-page spreads should include in the region of 1,000 words, selected by you. The opening spread must include images, introductory copy, and title detail, and the second spread should house the remaining copy and images. You must originate a masthead for *Arkitekt* magazine and apply this to the front cover together with other imagery and supporting text. The design systems you adopt must demonstrate scope so that the design solution can develop and function well for future issues of the magazine.

01 Client: Tria Properties
Design: Sayles Graphic Design

01

02 Client: Premios Principe Felipe
Design: Sonsoles Llorens

Methodology

Research

Firstly, investigate existing magazines that focus on the subject of architecture, architectural design, and interior design. Look at the magazines as they are displayed on the shelves of newsstands; consider the prominence and impact of their mastheads, assess their possible impact on the overall design of the magazine, and their appeal to the intended target audience. Think about possible formats, as well as different paper stocks and alternatives for binding.

Source sufficient appropriately structured text to use as the subject matter for your article. Make sure this text is hierarchically varied and includes details such as main headings, introductory copy, subheadings, text that can be used as captions or quotes, and copy that might be highlighted or accentuated within a box.

Research a range of imagery—photographs and/or drawings—that can be used to illustrate the selected text. Not only must these illustrate the article effectively, they must also sit well together and look as though they belong to the same set. Pay attention to the art direction, scale, and cropping to ensure that images have cohesion and scope.

Exploration and thumbnails

For the two double-page spreads, experiment with ways of bringing type and image together on layout sheets. Explore plenty of alternatives and trace the more successful solutions to refine your design options. Look for ways of bringing elements—text, headings, captions, and imagery—together through alignment, as this will help the future development of a grid system.

Having worked through various options, think about how much text is necessary for each of the spreads. It might be visually interesting to create a contrast by locating most of the text on one spread and using a mix of change of scale, use of space, and imagery on the other spread to give it a different character.

Render headings and larger type so that viewers of your roughs can read this level of information easily, even at this initial stage. Make sure that the tonal variations of body copy, captions, and other possible hierarchical variations are captured within thumbnail visuals. You should set the text with correct paragraph breaks and alignment.

Think about the fonts that might be used for this design. If you select more than one font, make sure there is a contrast between the families. Fonts that have a variety of weights are the most practical in an editorial context, as different weights can help communicate the levels of hierarchy within text.

In determining your page layout, don't start with the page frames and fit the detail to this. Instead, focus first on the groupings of type and image you would like and then impose page parameters, starting with the center margins and progressing to the page edges. Working this way round allows for different relationships of scale, and also for variation in the distribution of space within spreads. Make sure your thumbnails are in proportion to your desired format.

Source realistic text for the front cover. Look at the detail on the covers of actual magazines and ensure that the *Arkitekt* visual has credible detail. Having worked on the more complex double-page spreads, apply the same design relationships and systems to the front cover design. This will ensure that the cover design looks as though it belongs to the layout of the magazine.

Design development

In selecting the most successful design options for the spreads, analyze the alignments between elements in your thumbnails. You can use these alignments to form the basis of a grid structure that could be applied across both spreads, the front cover, and the rest of the magazine were it to be designed. To assess different grid options, consider the margins at the left- and right-hand edges of the pages. Think about margins at the center of the spreads; do they need to be slightly wider to accommodate the overall depth of the magazine and the type of binding used? The space between columns, known as the column gutter, needs to be wide enough to draw readers down the first column of text and prevent them reading across into the next column.

01 Client: *Plastique Magazine*
Design: Studio8 Design

01

02 Client: Royal Academy of Arts
Design: Studio8 Design

Selecting a grid system will help you translate your thumbnail designs into finished artwork. You can set up your grid in a page make-up program. The translation of thumbnail designs into actual layouts is demanding and time-consuming. One trick that helps with this is to either "photocopy up" or scan and enlarge your thumbnail designs to full size. You can then use these enlargements as a plan or pattern to follow when you bring together the elements and details that make up the double-page spread.

Remember to print out layouts at actual size regularly, as it is best to assess the strengths and weaknesses of a design from a printed version rather than relying on observations made on-screen which can be misleading. Stand back and assess the relationships created on the printed pages and cover.

Completion

Present your final spreads and cover design on medium-weight presentation boards ready to display in a print portfolio. Make sure the central fold of a double-page spread is visible. You could fix the cover design to the front cover of a magazine and then photograph this next to competing titles, or you could show it being read. Online presentation can also be a very practical way to display your design solutions, whether as a PDF or as separate digital images. Designs can be uploaded to personal or commercial portfolio sites.

There is a correlation between constructing buildings and designing a page or spread—parallels between the use of a grid structure to distribute text, image, and space and to fabricate a building can be drawn. The designs featured here show many examples of this.

01 Client: The Hellenic Centre

Design: With Relish

01

02

02 Client: Arup

Design: Studio8 Design

03 University of Ljubljana, Faculty of Law
Design: Krog

04 Client: Town & Country Planning (TCPA)
Design: thomas.matthews

Dynamically shaped buildings and patterns created from architectural fittings distinguish the pages in these layouts. A highly visible grid holds text and image together in a structured manner that fits the topic of this brief.

01 Client: United Business Media
Design: Studio8 Design

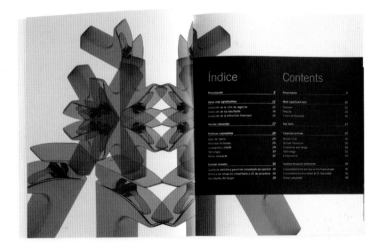

Solutions

Project: Magazine cover and spreads
Design: Leanne Pickering

Leanne Pickering has created a masthead that splits the word "arkitekt" in a manner reminiscent of building and construction, with main headings that also embrace this approach. She has added impact to her layouts through her use of the grid, assembling strong groupings that contain a variety of texture and tone, within both type and image.

The distinctive color palette used for all images has been carefully sourced from the front cover photograph, establishing another connection between pages.

"A full-color photograph can be a good source of color inspiration for type and graphics. This helps to ensure visual compatibility and association between the varied elements of a design."

Carolyn Knight and Jessica Glaser, Bright Pink

Project: Magazine cover and spreads
Design: Matt Zarandi

The concrete structure of one of the buildings in this magazine was the inspiration behind many of the unusual design decisions: cement is used as a background texture and the corners of graphic boxes are angled to reflect the decorative structure of the windows. The considered typographic detail—enlarged initial capital letters and changes in weight, scale, and column width—adds visual interest.

Project: Magazine cover and spreads
Design: David Healey

David Healey is particularly successful in echoing the form of a building with his typographic groupings in the spread below. He has also exploited change of pace to full advantage—his opening spread, which contains little text, is followed by a spread with a lot of text.

"The introduction of angled type can be eye-catching, but it is important to ensure that the angle is sufficiently acute to be seen as intentional and that this manipulation occurs more than once throughout a publication."

Jeff Leak, boing!

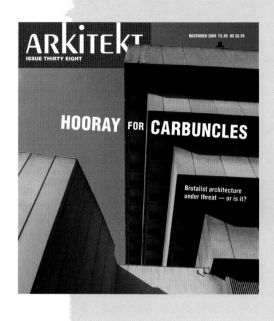

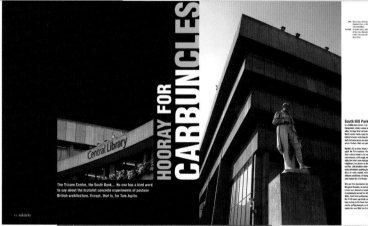

Project: Magazine cover and spreads
Design: Sigita Katiliute

Dynamically angled photographs characterize this design. They are complemented by the obvious horizontal and vertical emphasis of the type. The control of space, especially in the type-heavy spread, is particularly pleasing with the asymmetric balance achieved through the use of three columns on one page and two columns on the other. This is also enhanced by varied hanging points and line lengths. The typeface selected for the cover and main headings is comparatively angular and sits well with the treatment and content of the imagery.

Brief 02

● ● ○

Magazine cover, contents page & spreads

The brief

Design a minimum of three spreads, a cover, and a contents page for full-color, printed, weekly magazine *Promo*. This magazine covers topics including contemporary culture, art, drama, music, and twenty-first-century life

The brief explained

Target market

The target market for *Promo* magazine is over-25s with a youthful outlook and state of mind, a high level of disposable income, and a desire keep up to date with culture, art, music, and contemporary lifestyles. The magazine acts as a status symbol, informing onlookers that *Promo* readers are stylish, intelligent, and fashion-conscious.

Requirements

The spreads must be representative of the content and design of *Promo* magazine as a whole. All text and images must be sourced, allowing in the region of 1,000 words and a minimum of three images per double-page spread. When selecting copy, look for hierarchical differentiation in the form of introductory copy, main headings, quotes, and captions.

One of the spreads should contain a minimum of three small articles and should be given the sectional heading "*Promo* news." The exact format and size is left to your discretion, but it must work as part of an integral design concept that interprets at least some of the character, pace, and tone of your selected texts.

The design must include a front cover, contents page or spread, and masthead. The magazine style should be innovative and imaginative, without ignoring basic principles of hierarchy, composition, and legibility.

---

01 *Plastique Magazine*
Design: Studio8 Design

01

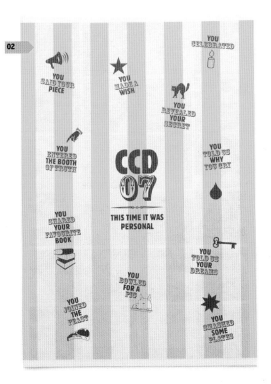

02 Client: Accenture Ireland
Design: Brighten The Corners

Methodology

Research

Take a look at the lifestyle magazines that proliferate today. Some come as supplements to weekend newspapers; others exist as standalone publications. Pay particular attention to the approach adopted by sections that contain a number of smaller articles under one heading. Look at the detail of contents pages and take particular note of how hierarchy is tackled. Look for recurring visual themes that develop through the pages of magazines and analyze how these provide publications with a distinct identity, but also scope for development of their design.

Examine the handling of imagery and observe cropping and changes of scale. In particular, look for any type that may be located on top of imagery or on colored backgrounds. How legible is this text? How have any problems with legibility been overcome? Are there any trends in magazine design worth noting? Any significant and relevant designs options that you could adopt, or avoid, for *Promo*?

Remember to source appropriate text for use in this visual. In selecting copy, read through carefully to make sure it allows sufficient scope for the creation of an interesting hierarchy. As you assess contemporary publications, keep sheets of layout paper and pencils to hand and make notes of memorable design details that could be relevant to the design of *Promo*. This is also the time to consider format, stock, and binding methods—the choices you make will help to create a distinctive identity for this new magazine.

Exploration and thumbnails

With your choice of text made, consider the possibilities for captions, quotes, introductory text, and highlighted copy. Work up rough visuals that provide proportionally accurate indications of combinations of type and image. These design possibilities need the right character to reach the intended *Promo* audience, and to be representative of the magazine design overall. To succeed in this, you will need to include examples of all the hierarchical relationships that may occur.

It is a good idea to discuss thumbnail designs with colleagues and other designers. Ask for opinions, point out areas of concern or special interest, and keep sheets of layout paper and pencils at hand to make notes and record developmental suggestions. It is surprising how often effective, unexpected design concepts can result from discussion with others.

In developing your design roughs, remember to think about establishing a grid structure for your magazine's layout. Look not only for vertical alignments, but also for horizontal alignments as these can help to provide a strong visual association between the left- and right-hand pages of a spread and subsequent pages.

Within your roughs, try to bring elements together in similar ways. For example, if two images have a corner-to-corner relationship, you could repeat this pattern within the spread and throughout the magazine. Possible design options might be to include similar corner-to corner relationships between the multiple lines of headings or text boxes containing body copy and captions.

Design development

Once you are happy with your design exploration and thumbnails, start incorporating computer-generated type and selected photographs or illustrations. It is difficult for even the most experienced designer to make the best, most effective translation from small-scale, hand-rendered thumbnails to screen by relying on visual judgments alone. The blank "page" presented by the bright screen of a monitor is undoubtedly enticing and flexible, but it can also be quite misleading, as scale and space can very easily be misjudged. "Photocopy up" or scan and enlarge your thumbnail designs to full size, then use these enlargements as a plan or pattern to follow in translating your design.

One of the most complex spreads in this brief is the contents page. Not only does this demand the sourcing of appropriately varied information, but it also provides the challenge of informing the reader, in an enticing manner, about the structure of the magazine in one glance. This is where a couple of contrasting fonts that include a variety of weights will prove to be most useful as typographic alternatives. Levels of importance can be stressed not only by changing face or weight, but also by changing case and size; leading and intercharacter spacing can also be very useful in creating informative textual and tonal variety.

As you work through computer-generated alternatives, be sure to print out pages at full size and assess them regularly. Check also for consistency of design elements such as rule sizes, margin widths, gutter sizes, paragraph breaks, and spaces between groups of elements; it is very easy to give these important design details more variety than you actually intend!

01 Client: Publishing and Design Group
Design: Studio8 Design

01

Completion

Print out your final cover design, contents, and double-page spreads and present them on neutral-colored, medium-weight presentation boards, or make up a "dummy" magazine that viewers can flick through. You will need to include a number of blank pages to bulk up the dummy to a realistic size. This method of presentation is especially effective for designs that involve the use of unusual paper stocks, page formats, and binding methods. Online presentation can also be a very practical way to display your design solutions, whether as a PDF or as separate digital images. Designs can be uploaded to personal or commercial portfolio sites. Small-scale typographic detail should be displayed carefully to ensure legibility.

02/03 Client: Publishing and Design Group
Design: Studio8 Design

03

All of these solutions have strong, characterful layouts carried throughout each page and section. Illustrative technique, style of photography, use of type, change of scale, color, grid structure, and distribution of space, all feature as powerful ways of personalizing the designs.

01 ▶

01 Client: Wolverhampton City Council
Design: Marie Campbell

02 Client: English Farming and Food Partnerships
Design: Purpose

03 Client: *Plastique Magazine*
Design: Studio8 Design

02 ▶

03 ▶

04

04 Client: Israeli Railways
Design: Oded Ezer

05

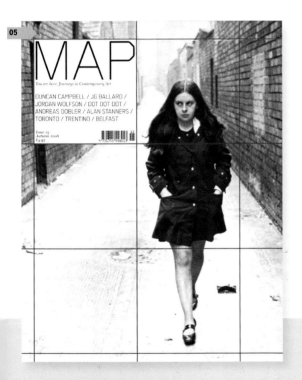

It is always pleasing to find examples of well-designed magazines that make considered use of materials, typographic texture and tone, imagery, groupings, composition, and color. You should source many varied publications for inspiration, but always be ready to distinguish between the mediocre and the more successful.

05 Client: *Map* Magazine
Design: Studio8 Design

Solutions

Project: Magazine cover, contents page, and spreads
Design: Selina Pal

A very individual illustrative style gives character to Selina Pal's design. The addition of a brown-paper texture and a patchwork of different typographic scales and weights creates memorable pages. Such styling is appropriate for a popular culture magazine, but don't underestimate the production time and the amount of effort necessary to achieve this result.

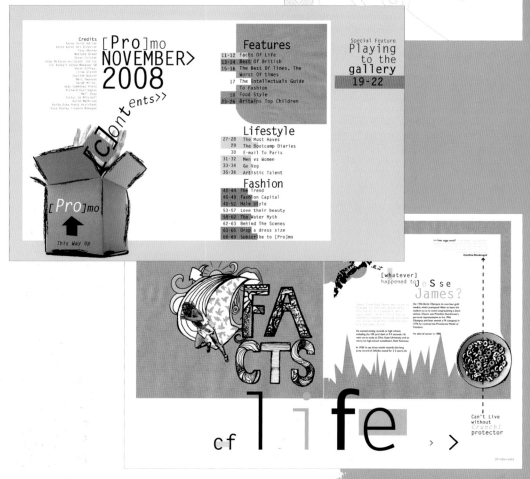

Project: Magazine cover, contents page, and spreads
Design: Wayde Raphael

The reader's eyes are drawn across these two spreads by lively letterforms and imagery that both have a subtle directional emphasis. Viewed at 100%, Wade Raphael's large type is dynamic, but this is lost a little through the reduction of the page size for printing. The octagonal element is particularly evident within display type and image boxes, and as this feature appears throughout the design, it helps to maintain continuity.

Project: Magazine cover, contents page, and spreads
Design: Anette Mosdøl

Strong colors, circular shapes, and dynamic use of space are a strong feature in Anette Mosdøl's interpretation of *Promo* magazine. Even the letterforms of the namestyle appear to be constructed from circles. Tight, restrained blocks of type come together with consistently applied subheadings and this contrasts nicely with the effusive, bubbly shapes.

"I like to add visual texture and tone to body typography, extracting quotes or enticing texts to ensure that an audience finds my designs interesting and enjoyable. The choice of a font that enables a great variety of alternatives in terms of typographic texture and tone allows for the effective handling of complex hierarchies."

Jeff Leak, boing!

Project: Magazine cover, contents page, and spreads
Design: Aneesa Iqbal

A bright color palette augmented by decorative smoke patterns and linear imagery distinguishes Aneesa Iqbal's *Promo* pages. The typographic detailing of the headings, along with their vertical orientation, complements the staggered columns of text. A clear hierarchy is established through the use of white text reversed through colored blocks, and this also adds interest to the page. Cut-out imagery contributes to the dynamic style of this design, as the shapes created are more impactful than neatly framed alternatives.

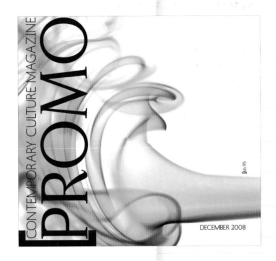

Project: Magazine cover, contents page, and spreads
Design: Vanesha Parmar

In many magazines type is bland and uninviting; this is not the case with Vanesha Parmar's design. Headings, subheadings, and highlighted copy work hierarchically to provide a number of levels of engagement, while unusually shaped columns and image boxes introduce a real sense of visual excitement. Although inside pages have extremely good cohesion, it is interesting to note that the cover design and masthead are set in a different typeface.

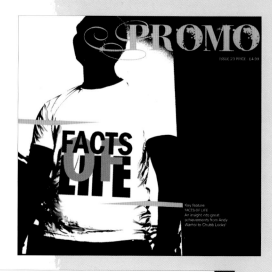

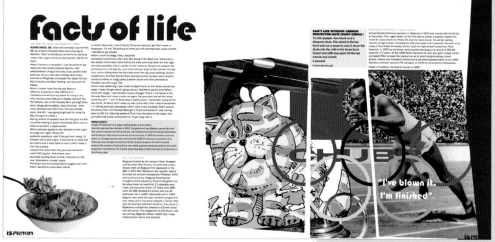

PLAYING TO THE GALLERY
FEATURE SOPHIE LERIS PHOTOGRAPHS PAUL MASSEY

THE INTELLECTUAL'S GUIDE TO FASHION

"Although subtle shaping of text boxes, as in Vanesha Parmar's work, is a pleasing development of design systems, extreme shaping, such as forcing text into a triangular or more figurative form, creates many problems. This will inevitably result in uncomfortable and ugly spacing between words and problematic hyphenations, both of which will reduce legibility."

Carolyn Knight and Jessica Glaser, Bright Pink

Brief 03

●●●

Arts program

The brief

Design sample spreads, cover, and contents pages for a promotional arts program

The brief explained

Target market

The target audience for this arts program is likely to vary according to your selected event: enthusiasts of artistic disciplines could range in age from 16 to 85+, they could be male or female and from any background. However, one definite is that the target audience will have some disposable income available to spend on enjoying and supporting arts entertainment and education.

01 Client: The Gate Theatre
Design: Rose Design

Requirements

The pages must communicate the essence of a festival or extensive arts-focused event or celebration. They must be full color and representative of the design of the program overall. All text and images must be sourced, allowing in the region of 300 words and a minimum of three images per double-page spread. The exact format and size is left to your discretion. The selected arts event, real or imaginary, must provide an exciting opportunity for the practitioners and/or performers to showcase their talents; your design concepts should reflect the atmosphere, style, appeal, and innovation of the event. Text must include listings for each event, providing the reader with such detail as titles, timings, prices, a brief description, reviews, location and production information, and sponsorship details if relevant. To cope with this level of hierarchical complexity and ensure scope within design groupings and page layout, you must develop a detailed design style that will ensure continuity in the program, while also allowing for flexibility and variety within individual pages.

02 Client:
Philharmonia
Orchestra
Design: With Relish

You will need to make many decisions during the research stage of this project. These include considerations of format, use of materials, binding methods, and selection of appropriate print techniques. If the chosen event is divided into a number of themed sections or groups of connected performances, consider how best to present the program. Is it a good idea to simply set all information together, or should sections be used to subdivide it? Should this program be one physical item of print, or should it be composed of a number of visually associated, but separate elements, held together in one package?

Methodology

Research

There are many arts events and festivals that take place throughout the year, each focusing on a distinct topic and each appealing to a different audience. Look into these events, examine their publicity material, and pay particular attention to commemorative programs that provide the audience not only with visuals of the event and images of participants, but also with details of performances, exhibitions, and other public presentations. Many celebratory programs are kept as mementos. It is not uncommon for these programs to have an unusual format and method of binding, an unexpected print technique, or another memorable design surprise.

Spend time choosing the subject for the program and source the relevant copy, making sure that there is hierarchical variety. It is very likely that the finished visual will include a number of similarly written listings. Although in one respect this may come across as being somewhat visually repetitive, it does offer a good opportunity to devise appealing and recognizable systems that allow for scope and variety, as well as detectable visual consistency.

Exploration and thumbnails

Having decided upon the format, theme, and content for this project, it is time to begin recording design options as thumbnails. Start with the most complex area of the design, as this will ensure that you establish visual systems that are able to cope with any design eventuality presented by this complex project. A page containing a number of event listings is likely to provide one of the most difficult areas of this challenge. You need to develop flexible design systems that present many levels of information clearly. If each listing is presented with the same configuration, the pages will all be very similar to one another and the overall program will lack vitality.

Using layout or marker paper is an excellent way to explore variations on a theme, as you can trace designs and experiment with bringing elements together in many different ways before settling on final options. This design project provides an ideal vehicle for considering uncommon print techniques such as the use of special colors, unusual folding techniques, and unexpected formats.

If the design involves section breaks or dividers, consider how these divisions will be indicated. What would be the best way to mark these changes? One of the most common methods of indicating a change of topic is to adopt a change of color palette, or to include a distinctively styled divider page.

In an editorial layout it is not only type that requires a hierarchy, texture, and tone—the images used also need a strong visual hierarchy to lead the reader from picture to picture. Color value, tonal intensity, scale, and textural detail all play important roles in the creation of an image-based hierarchy; a dark-toned, large-scale photograph is likely to attract the attention of the audience, but the expertise of the designer can then draw their attention to other images in a desired sequence.

Design development

Having created a number of successful hand-generated visuals and sought the opinions of valued colleagues, begin developing your design ideas on screen. In interpreting your thumbnail designs, make sure you don't overlook subtleties of space, scale, and tonal variation, or your computer-generated versions will disappoint. Throughout the design development process check full-size printouts to ensure that all the hierarchical and tonal relationships are as you desired.

If the final design involves the use of an unusual format or unexpected folding or binding systems, make up a dummy to check that these production processes will work as you expect.

01 Client: Royal Mail
Design: Rose Design

Join
the
party

Come to the BFI's 75th Birthday party this September and celebrate with us in style. In London, across the UK and online there are many ways to join in.
www.bfi.org.uk/75

BFI 75 – Visions for the Future
Cate Blanchett, Simon Pegg, Bill Nighy, Matt Lucas and Sir Ben Kingsley are amongst 75 people who have chosen their film for the future. See their choices and vote for your own.
www.bfi.org.uk/75

Films

Events

Ways
to join in...

Download 75 films for 75 pence

Enter the Time Machine to discover film at BFI Southbank

Travel through time at the BFI 'Back to the Future' Weekender

Party all night at the BFI IMAX

Celebrate at home with a special BFI 75 DVD box set

www.bfi.org.uk/75

From the BFI
National Archive

To enjoy
at home

Displays

In the Gallery

www.bfi.org.uk/75

02/03 Client: BFI (British Film Institute)
Design: Rose Design

Completion

If part of the experience of reading this arts program involves its unusual format or structure, the most effective way of presenting this visual is to make up a 3D dummy so that readers of your print-based portfolio can enjoy interacting with the pages. It might be necessary to include some blank pages to bulk out the body of the design. Online presentation can also be a very practical way to display your design solutions, whether as a PDF or as separate digital images. Designs can be uploaded to personal or commercial portfolio sites. Small-scale typographic detail should be displayed carefully to ensure legibility.

This project demands lively and exciting pages with the option of an unusual construction. These designs show a range of formats. Three of the examples use type as image—a pleasing alternative to photography or illustration.

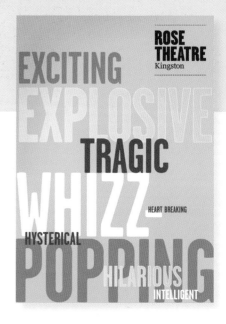

This series of vibrant designs provides ideal inspiration for an arts program. Take note of the recurring colors, shapes, patterns, and styles and how they have been used to hold covers and pages together as parts of a whole. Even if these were scattered randomly across the spread, it would not be difficult to determine family groupings.

04 Client: University College Falmouth
Design: ArthurSteen-HorneAdamson

05 Client: Philharmonia Orchestra
Design: With Relish

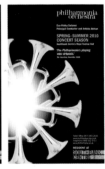

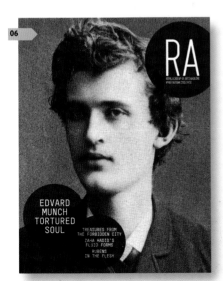

06 Client: Royal Academy of Arts
Design: Studio8 Design

Solutions

Project: Arts program
Design: Caroline Kruse Pettersson

On the macro level, lively colors and cut-out images define Caroline Kruse Pettersson's program for The Edinburgh Fringe Festival; on the micro level, interesting relationships of typographic hierarchy and careful compositional detailing combine to produce a visually enticing publication and a highly informative piece. Bright colors and carefully selected patterns and images are used to reinforce the quirky, humorous nature of the event to great effect.

Project: Arts program
Design: Vanesha Parmar

The slabs of color used on the front cover to code the
four main venues for the Edinburgh Fringe Festival
become signature colors for the sections relating to
each location. Vanesha Parmar controls the text-heavy
pages skillfully by breaking the information down
into different levels and groupings. The introductory
spread for the Gilded Balloon uses six variations of type,
excluding the headings, and succeeds in producing
a lively, accessible, and cohesive spread.

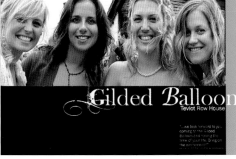

08

35

Project: Arts program
Design: Aneesa Iqbal

In Aneesa Iqbal's spreads a memorable color palette, which includes full-color images and carefully chosen areas of flat color, is used to represent each venue. Typographic groupings formed through different orientations, weights, and colors ensure that the information for each event is visually clear and easy to understand.

"As the Edinburgh Fringe is a particularly lively and vibrant event, it is essential that this is communicated through the style of the design in order for these spreads to succeed. Cut-out images are always more dynamic than squared-up images."

Carolyn Knight and Jessica Glaser, Bright Pink

Project: Arts program
Design: Grace Oakley

Grace Oakley adopted a very distinctive approach for her program design: strong background colors "splattered" with contrasting paint spots, and high contrast, single-color, illustrative portraits are key elements of this design. On each page the color combinations have been selected to set up a strobing effect in order to create a mnemonic design. Note that there is no white used in the design—this reduces the range of tonal depth and contrast on the pages.

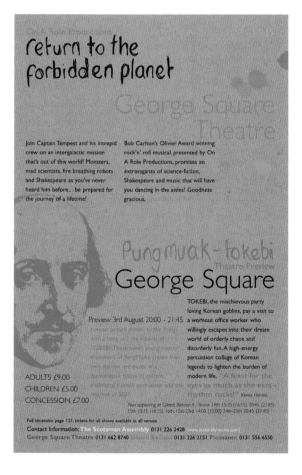

Project: Arts program
Design: Jashmita Patel

Jashmita Patel has used a palette of shapes and colors to categorize the different venues and a distinctive display font to provide a consistent link throughout her program design. She has used her flexible grid structure to good effect, controlling image and text in a varied and lively, yet consistent manner. She has established a successful typographic hierarchy through shifts in color and scale.

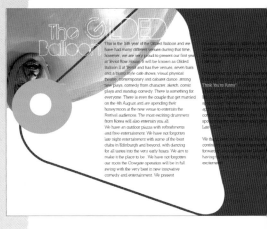

36

> "Grouping elements in a page layout to allow space to run around type and image often creates more powerful designs. Spacing elements evenly across a page tends to weaken any system of hierarchy and because of this, to result in a less dynamic composition."

Carolyn Knight and Jessica Glaser, Bright Pink

RETURN TO THE FORBIDDEN PLANET
15:20 (17:45) On A Role Productions
George Square Theatre
Preview 3rd Aug £4 £8.00 (£6.00)

"Ladies and Gentlemen, on behalf of the Captain and his crew, we would like to welcome you aboard Scientific Survey Flight Nine". Join Captain Tempest and his intrepid crew on an intergalactic mission that's out of this world! Monsters, mad scientists, fire breathing robots and Shakespeare as you've never heard him before, be prepared for the journey of a lifetime! Bob Carlton's Olivier Award winning rock 'n' roll musical, presented by On A Role Productions, promises an extravaganza of science fiction, Shakespeare and music that will have you dancing in the aisles! Goodness gracious, Great Balls of Fire!

SOUNDS OF TOKEBI
20:40 (21:45) PungMuAk - Tokebi
George Square Theatre Preview 3rd Aug
£5 £9.00 (£7.00)

Korean culture comes to the Fringe with a bang and the sounds of TOKEBI! These seven young master drummers of PungMuAk create their own rhythm and music in a spontaneous fusion of ancient traditional Korean percussion and the rhythms of 2001. TOKEBI, the mischievous party loving Korean goblins, pay a visit to a wornout office worker who willingly escapes into their dream world of orderly chaos and disorderly fun. A high-energy percussion collage of Korean legends to lighten the burden of modern life.

"A feast for the eyes as much as the ears ... rhythm rocks!" Korea Herald.

Also appearing at Gilded Balloon II - Teviot
14th 15:15 (16:15) 20:45 (21:45)
15th 15:15 (16:15)
16th, 15st-23rd 14:00 (15:00)
24th-25th 20:45 (21:45)

Section 04
Music
graphics

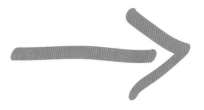

Graphics for the music industry need to appeal to a wide range of tastes. While the exercises in this section give you an opportunity to engage with a number of styles of music, they don't attempt to embrace every genre or appeal to every taste. However, the research imagery included explores a rich diversity in approach, and the exercises should prove a valuable introduction to this popular graphic design discipline.

Since the turn of the twenty-first century many changes have taken place in the world of music, with downloads replacing many CD sales and vinyl covers becoming more of a niche market. As a consequence, designers face a considerable challenge to create exciting designs that will work in many contexts.

As Rob O'Connor of Stylorouge says, "Design for music has traditionally been seen as the sleeve image. This is changing due to the increasing download market, but a visual campaign still needs a core focal point that assumes the role of the record sleeve: the thumbnails for iTunes, the banner web ads, etc." Although, in many respects, the visual identity of music now has to fight for prominence, if a designer can create striking, emotive designs or imagery, the visual presence of an artist or artists can have a huge impact on audience awareness, leading to greater popularity and more sales. Rob O'Connor continues, "It [music design] is still only effective as part of a complete campaign to address potential markets. Tapping into the visual zeitgeist is something of a holy grail for music marketeers as designs have to give an artist or project the appearance of being the height of cool and fashion without losing any individuality."

01 Client: Warner Music Philippines
Design: Inksurge

02 Client: Pearl Jam
Design: Ames Bros

Trying to capture the essence of a piece of music in visual form can be a good starting point for music graphics. If a designer is immersed in the sound and lyrics of an artist or performer, this can inspire images which can then be developed to make up the basis of appropriate design work. Asked to describe his favored method of beginning a new design project, Rob O'Connor replies, "Left to my own devices, I would say that my usual approach is to immerse myself in the music, read the lyrics, research the artist and the musical genre, then build up a notebook of thoughts, sketches, tearsheets from books and magazines, and images downloaded from the web. The items collected will often work both with and against each other to inspire some original thoughts of my own. I always discuss my ideas with my colleagues at Stylorouge. Collaboration is an essential part of the way we work. Our thoughts are generally distilled into a few visuals and written proposals that we then leave for a day or two to revisit, with a degree of objectivity, before we present them to a client."

Peter Crnokrak, of The Luxury of Protest, gives a different view. He says, "Some designers might say one should do research into the target market/audience and work out a design solution that is appropriate. Although this approach may work, when it comes to expressive and poetic work, as is common for the music industry, an out-of-the-box, atypical approach is most likely to be attention-grabbing and, therefore, most successful." Music and artwork are seen by many as inseparable, and an iconic cover is likely to stay in the mind as long as the music itself. It is often an image that provides a first introduction to a type of music, band, or artist, and this could be in the form of a prominently displayed poster, or even a T-shirt worn by a passerby. As far as the designer is concerned, although the platforms for communicating the visual identity of performers or music have changed, its role is as significant today as it ever has been. Peter Crnokrak says, "I've always viewed music graphics in the same light as identity development for a general client. In both cases, the key to success is to appeal to the emotions by creating a visual that draws the viewer's attention and holds it."

Music is an immensely popular subject and an integral part of the lives of many people. As a result, it is not surprising that many graphic designers aspire to working within this extremely competitive field. Many well-known music designers have different ideas and recommendations concerning how best to break into designing for music merchandise. Jason Munn of The Small Stakes believes that "It is important to get involved with your local music scene. Try to find bands that you could do work for. This not only benefits the local scene, but also gives you an opportunity to build up a body of work."

01 Client: Brittain Ashford
Design: Samia Saleem

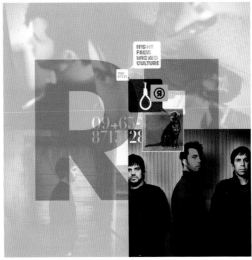

Peter Crnokrak is of the opinion that "One of the best ways to get into design for music is to prove your worth by showing the artists themselves what your skills are. Instead of simply sending examples of one's portfolio out for viewing, design specific promotional material for artists on a speculative basis. I'd also recommend designing for up-and-coming bands which, typically, have little money to invest in music graphics as opposed to established acts that are likely to ignore you. Be proactive and send your work to the artists themselves rather than the record label that represents them. If *they* like your work, your chance of success is much higher."

Whether it is good to work speculatively is always debatable, whatever the area of design or the type of client; some designers feel that doing work free diminishes the value of the graphic design profession. Rob O'Connor advises not to work for nothing. "Don't take on any old freelance job to get a foot in the door unless you are absolutely sure it will benefit you and that you'll get paid! Try to get some experience with a company that specializes in the area of music, but be prepared to find something to enjoy in every project."

The most important thing to do is to build up a portfolio of designs that demonstrate your skill, enthusiasm, and aptitude for music graphics. The exercises here could prove an excellent springboard into this area of the graphic design profession and the supplied methodologies give you a reliable way of working for any future projects. It is rare for a designer to work exclusively within the realms of their favorite style of music or for their favorite group, so a portfolio that displays breadth and diversity is likely to be the most appealing and successful.

02 Client: Tooth & Nail Records
Design: Invisible Creature

Glossary

alignment the arrangement of image and text in a design, typically from a left, right, central, top, or bottom axis

crop to select a specific area of an image and cut out (crop) unwanted areas

elements of design the building blocks of design: color, shape, size, space, line, value, and texture

genre an artistic type or style; an area of expertise

hierarchy (visual hierarchy) the arrangement of elements to guide viewers through them in a specific order

house style a visual identity that links everything related to a company or to a performer or performers

identity palette the visual elements that come together to form an identity; an identity palette can be used much like an artist's palette, with elements used in various combinations

jewel case the plastic case that holds a CD with its cover and paper insert

logo/logotype distinctive visual character created by the design of the letters that constitute a product name; a namestyle

marker paper specialist flimsy paper with a coating that prevents marker pens from bleeding through to surfaces below

mark-making the process of applying pen or pencil to paper; the character of marks made by different implements or technological effects

mnemonic assisting or intending to assist memory

namestyle see logo/logotype

onomatopoeic having a sound that suggests the meaning of the word

out of the box innovative and unusual

sleeve open-ended slipcase, usually for a vinyl record

spatial distribution organization of image and space

stylized font a typeface that is representative of a particular period or genre; stylized fonts tend to be elaborate

symbol a distinctive image or mark that represents a product; generally works with a namestyle

system (design system) the criteria used for organizing different elements in relation to each other to form a considered whole

tearsheets relevant and inspiring pages or sections of pages torn from publications

thumbnails comparatively small rough visuals that incorporate sufficient detail and accuracy to be of value for decision-making

visual code/visual cue visual element or group of elements that have a definite connotation due to frequency of use in similar situations

visual language a meaningful language created by visual elements other than words

visual zeitgeist the style of image and fashion that is characteristic of the moment

Reading list

Airside
Airside

CD-Art: Innovation in CD
Packaging Design
Charlotte Rivers

Contemporary Album Cover
Design
Max Dax

Graphis Poster Annual 08/09
Martin Pederson

Non-Format Love Song
Kjell Ekhorn and Jon Forss

Print + Production Finishes
for CD + DVD Packaging
Loewy

Sonic: Visuals for Music
Hendrick Hellige and Robert Klanten

Supersonic: Visuals for Music
Hendrick Hellige and Robert Klanten

Equipment

- Scalpel
- Marker paper
- Pencils
- Markers/colored pencils
- Steel ruler
- Set square
- Typeface reference
- Cutting mat
- Double-sided tape
- Low-tack adhesive tape
- Adhesive tape
- Spray adhesive
- Lightweight card
- Professional color-matching reference
- Computer/software

Brief 01

CD covers

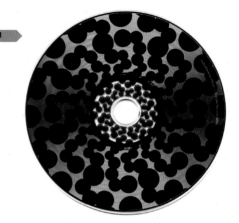

01

The brief

Design a series of front covers for CDs of modern classical music, or a modern interpretation of classical music

The brief explained

Target market

The target audience for this brief is music enthusiasts with an interest in classical and contemporary interpretations of classical scores. Although a percentage of young people studying music may wish to purchase these CDs, the majority of consumers with an interest in the modern classics are likely to be older than 25 and to have an extensive knowledge of music.

Requirements

The series must have a seasonal theme. Designs should reflect the pace and mood of the music and persuade shoppers to buy. Each cover should work on its own and as part of the set of three; the set must display cohesion and variety. You may design the cover for real or fictitious music or artists.

02

01 Client: Radical Fashion, Hetty Records
Design: BankerWessel

02 Client: Croatian National Tourist Board
Design: Studio International

Methodology

Research

Familiarize yourself not only with existing CDs in the contemporary classical music genre, but also with a range of contemporary design concepts for different music genres. Listen to a range of music, as this will help you establish the style and mood you wish to explore in your design. Only the front covers have to be designed; take note of the amount of information generally included on front covers, along with the size of type, and the kind of imagery used.

As the CDs are to form a set with a seasonal theme, research imagery and typefaces that are reminiscent of each of the seasons. Art galleries and books on contemporary artists are both excellent resources, or you could always take your inspiration directly from nature.

If the music selected is to be played by a specific musician, group, or orchestra, look into the style and character of the artist(s). Do they have a unique appearance or do they play unusual instruments? Do they have a recognized musical heritage, or are they renowned for any particular achievement?

Exploration and thumbnails

Experiment with a range of mark-making materials and implements to capture different moods and atmospheres. The style and technique you choose will play a vital role in communicating the essence of the music and the seasonal theme. Gouache, crayons, watercolors, pencils, charcoal, and collage are all possible options for interpreting imagery and capable of creating very different characteristics. Scanning hand-generated imagery and manipulating detail on-screen can be an intriguing and valuable method of developing design options, and also of generating unexpected results. Experiment with unusual color combinations and try to avoid predictable relationships of hues. You can change color emphasis, temperature, and priority quickly and easily on-screen to give a complete shift in meaning. You could also source or take photos yourself. The range of possible subject matter is vast, from figurative shots of people or landscapes, to patterns created by close-ups, and abstract shots dominated by technique.

Concepts could be purely typographic, although this would probably involve the introduction of some additional type. You could interpret descriptive or onomatopoeic words that suggest the style of music through different fonts, scales, and arrangements that emphasize their meanings.

03

04

03 Client: Tooth & Nail Records
Design: Invisible Creature

04 Client: Promotone B.V.
Design: Stefan Sagmeister

Design development

Explore as many concepts as possible. Begin by producing a range of hand-drawn roughs, bringing type and image together in the correct scale. Group all the visual elements before imposing a frame so as to enable more scope and dynamism in composition. Scan some of the textures and imagery you created in your roughs and combine them with type on the computer. Don't just focus on the imagery; consider where and how the type will sit. Any imagery should be selected bearing in mind the treatment and position of the type, not only to avoid problems with legibility, but also to make the most of alignments between letterforms and significant elements within the image.

Remember that each cover needs to function independently and as part of the set of three. Don't work on any one cover in isolation, but constantly refer to the detail of all three.

Completion

Your final design solutions can be presented in a number of ways. Computer printouts can be cut to size and mounted on neutrally colored, medium-weight card that will fit into your selected print portfolio. Another option is to make up 3D versions of the designs, either by inserting your covers into clear plastic jewel cases, or by making up card mock-ups. You can then photograph these 3D models, individually and in a group, and display prints in your portfolio. Online presentation can also be a very practical way to display your design solutions, whether as a PDF or as separate digital images. Designs can be uploaded to personal or commercial portfolio sites.

As well as looking at CD covers, look at the booklets inside the jewel case. These can be very helpful with design for music. The manner in which pages relate to each other can be just as inspirational as the way several covers work together.

01 Client: Croatian National Tourist Board
Design: Studio International

02 Client: Warner Bros.

Design: Stefan Sagmeister

03 Client: Wall of Sound

Design: Studio8 Design

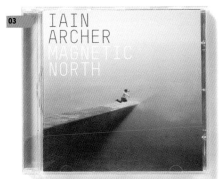

04 Client: Hetty
Records

Design: BankerWessel

The work displayed here provides inspiration for subject matter, technique, mark-making, and use of innovative print processes. Although it isn't required by the brief, it is possible to consider involving the use of eye-catching print and production techniques.

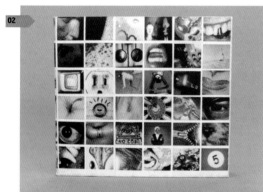

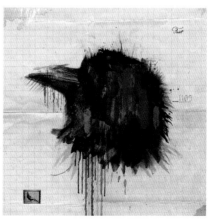

IVORYLINE
THERE
CAME
A
LION

01 Client: Capitol Records
Design: Stefan Sagmeister

02 Client: Pearl Jam
Design: Ames Bros

03 Client: Tooth & Nail Records
Design: Invisible Creature

04

MAINSTAY
BECOME
WHO YOU ARE

05

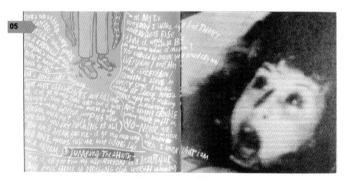

FAR-LESS

06

NO such thing

FINALLY FOREVER / SILENCE THE VOICES

04 Client: BEC
Recordings
Design: Invisible
Creature

05 Client: Tooth &
Nail Records
Design: Invisible
Creature

06 Client:
Interscope Records
Design: Invisible
Creature

Solutions

Project: CD covers
Design: Jeff Leak

Monochrome backgrounds of controlled, geometric patterns are overlaid with contrasting, random, abstract scribbles with a view to capturing the essence of these classical favorites with a modern interpretation. The backgrounds suggest the well-known harmonies and themes, while the free spirit of the lines represents the extemporizing that gives them a different twist. The result is a new and clean visual interpretation, and the vertical lines of type have a contemporary feel. The color of each cover is different from the others because, although they are part of a set, they contain music from very different composers.

Project: CD covers
Design: Ben Kelly

Striking illustrations of stylized winter landscapes dominate this collection. They give a sense of an ethereal atmosphere that reflects the contemporary nature of these recordings. The sophisticated manner in which the letterforms play on the color of the people in the images reflects the interplay of instruments and the sensitive and fresh interpretations of the music on the CDs. It could be argued that the fine type is not entirely legible when printed at a small size, but it is evident that the designer wanted to retain a fine balance between the hierarchy of type and image, and bold type might have been too powerful.

"Music graphics for existing artists are only one part of the process of creating an image for music. Design for music is unique inasmuch as the 'product' is a human being, with a personality and a potentially high public profile. The two end up being considered as part of a whole. TV appearances, promo videos, news articles, music packaging, and advertising—all of them combine to affect the market's perception of the person/product."

Rob O'Connor, Stylorouge

Project: CD covers
Design: Jeff Leak

The minimalist approach to this set of CD designs creates a visual language that suggests the music is contemporary in style. Smooth, painterly backgrounds, mostly in cold, icy colors, link with consistently positioned small type. The restrained and unusual treatment of all elements implies that the musical interpretations are likely to be out of the ordinary.

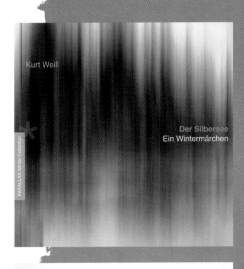

Project: CD covers
Design: Bright Pink

This set of covers gives a clear indication of the lighter, more accessible nature of the music they contain through the use of the familiar snowflake icon and larger, "friendly" typography.

"Be true to the peculiar requirements of the project, but don't rule out what, at first, you think might not be right for it. Challenging a convention is the mother of innovation. If you have a good understanding of the music in question, and a general respect for music and visual arts, you will know what you feel works and what doesn't."

Rob O'Connor, Stylorouge

paralux winter collection 2009

serge prokofieff

winter bonfire

symphony #7

morten lauridsen

midwinter songs

polyphony

paralux winter collection 2009

se winter a r in

john taven

hymn to the mother of god

Brief 02

Promotional posters

The brief
Design a series of three promotional posters for a real or fictitious artist or band

The brief explained
Target market
With this brief you are required to select the most appropriate target audience for your chosen artist or band; this involves careful analysis and consideration of the age range, gender, and lifestyle of the audience. For example, if this music is part of a lifestyle choice then you will have to take the impact of "style tribe" details into account.

Requirements
The posters must promote three different tours and/or albums. The designs must capture the style of the artist(s) and their music and convey this to the intended audience. Designs should feature information including the name of the artist or band, the name of the album or tour, the logo of the music publisher, and any performance details.

01 Client: Philadelphia Youth Orchestra
Design: Paone Design Associates

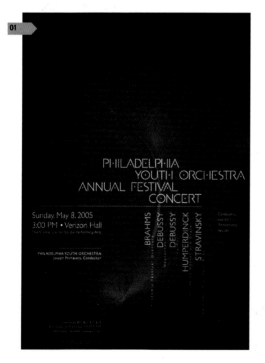

02 Client: Metro Arts Alliance
Design: Sayles Graphic Design

Methodology

Research

Research the style and character of your chosen artist. You will need to spend time listening to tracks and reading any available articles in magazines or on the Internet.

There is a sense in which "anything goes" in the design of posters for the music industry. It could be argued, therefore, that it is necessary to look at an even larger range of examples than for other designs in order to really get a feel for the project. The music business involves all levels of skill and talent and the standards of posters produced for the industry reflect this. As part of your research, look at posters of all standards. Recognizing poor design will be just as valuable as admiring successful designs; it will flag up what to avoid and what to take into consideration.

A poster needs to be read from some distance away, so look into what fonts and point sizes will give the most legible type, which colors and combinations of colors are the most eye-catching, and what positioning of elements will have the most impact. It would also be useful to find out where music posters are usually displayed. Are yours to be viewed in isolation, or will they appear alongside lots of other posters? Will they be used in repetitive displays, showing 20 or more of the same poster?

Your research for this project should include the differences between classical and contemporary music posters, or posters aimed at audiences above or below 25, as such details will help you reach your target market. If, for example, certain visual codes "speak" more successfully to over-25s, any designs for that market must take them into consideration.

Exploration and thumbnails

Many people visualize pictures or images when they listen to music; some also identify sounds, rhythms, and passages with specific colors. Listen to the music that is to be promoted in your posters and try to capture, on paper, any images, shapes, or colors that are triggered in your mind: they could form a good starting point for your designs. If there are lyrics to the music, you could base the design of your posters on these. Mark-making techniques could be very significant in this project: particular marks can represent specific instruments or voices. Listen carefully to the music and experiment with various pigments and implements.

While the posters can be for albums and/or concerts, all three must look as though they belong to a set, so even at the experimentation stage it is important to conceive ideas that have scope. Look at which aspects of the designs you could use to establish a connection between each poster, from similarity of subject matter to the style of type or image, and the intensity of color. Typefaces can be very expressive within posters as, generally, a few words are depicted at a sufficiently large scale for the nuances of shape and detail to convey quite specific character and style. Render the main heading in comparatively large letterforms, in a number of fonts, and assess their appropriateness.

Bear in mind that certain genres of music are synonymous with particular stylized fonts, but experiment and make your own judgment as to whether such a convention should be respected.

Your experiments should provide you with a kind of palette of elements from which to pick and choose in order to create thumbnails. To begin, group your chosen elements to set up harmonious alignments, spatial distribution, and relationships of scale. Do this before you impose an outer frame. Drawing up a series of correctly proportioned boxes that then have to be filled is really limiting in terms of composition. Not only is it difficult to achieve precise locations and dynamic contrasts of scale when drawing freehand in a small area, your designs will be considerably less predictable if you impose different-sized frames in different positions at the end of the process. With any design, from the moment any one element—a word, a line, an image—is placed on the marker paper, everything else has to be placed and sized in relation to that. Distances, angles, shapes, mark-making, and tonal values must all relate to each other either.

The main task of a poster is to attract the attention of a passing audience, so it is essential that not too much information is included. The main image and/or text should have a dynamic configuration that catches the eyes of passersby and pulls them in if the subject is of interest to them. Coming closer, they can read any remaining copy, which need not be set at more than 12pt on an average-size poster.

At this stage you should generate a minimum of six potential ideas for each poster. They could all be visualized on marker paper, or they could involve some computer work to explore certain typefaces or found imagery.

Design development
Select the strongest concept from your thumbnails and take it up to full size. Photocopying small visuals in black-and-white can be an easy and efficient way to flag up the strengths and weaknesses of a layout. Look at how all your design decisions work within each poster and how they relate to each of the other posters. Finally, produce the posters on-screen at actual size so that you can print them out. You will need to view certain areas of the posters at 100% to check detailing, but much of each poster can be viewed as a whole on-screen.

Completion
There is no doubt that full-size printouts of your final poster designs would look the most impressive within a print portfolio. However, smaller-scale versions are acceptable and can provide a dynamic contrast of scale when displayed next to a larger piece. This method of presentation has the added advantage of allowing all posters to be seen together, as a set. Mount your final solutions on neutral-colored, medium-weight card. Online presentation can also be a very practical way to display your design solutions, whether as a PDF or as separate digital images. Designs can be uploaded to personal or commercial portfolio sites.

01

01 Client: Philharmonia Orchestra
Design: With Relish

In a number of these designs the character of image and type is amalgamated and there is a real sense of coherence. It is important to treat image and text either in a similar way or in a distinct and contrasting manner so that they don't compete visually.

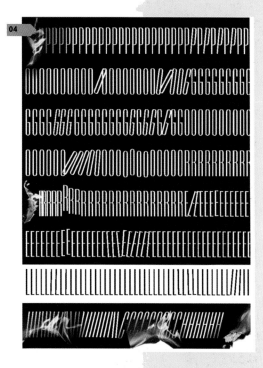

02 Client:
Philadelphia Youth
Orchestra
Design: Paone Design
Associates

03 Client: Rough
Trade Records
Design: The Luxury
of Protest

04 Client: Rotary
Club Zagreb
Design: Studio
International

05 Client: Warner
Brothers Music
Design: Stefan
Sagmeister

tHe
BABYSHAMBLES SESSiONS
1, 2 & 3

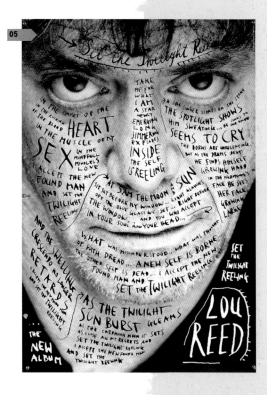

The posters on this spread are typical of the work of The Small Stakes. The detailing and thought processes involved in the creation of these designs show a unique and recognizable character. Although they are individual pieces, their similarity creates an identifiable family.

02

01
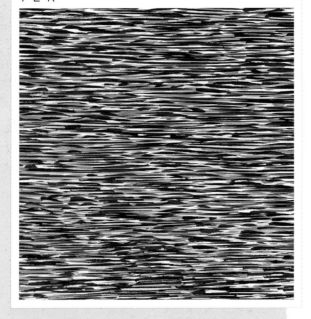

03

01 Client: Deerhunter
Design: The Small Stakes

02 Client: Rilo Kiley
Design: The Small Stakes

03 Client: Nada Surf
Design: The Small Stakes

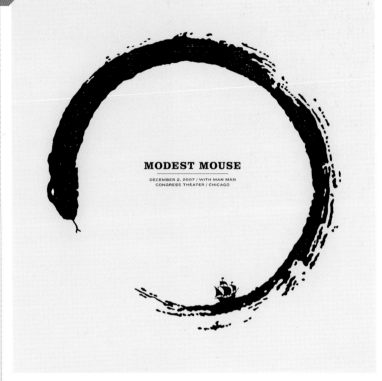

MODEST MOUSE

DECEMBER 2, 2007 / WITH MAN MAN
CONGRESS THEATER / CHICAGO

04 Client: Modest Mouse
Design: The Small Stakes

05 Client: Broken Social Scene
Design: The Small Stakes

05

BROKEN SOCIAL SCENE
MANCHESTER ACADEMY FEBRUARY 14 £8.50

Significant areas of flat color can be very useful design devices in posters as they create powerful and attention-grabbing tonal and compositional values. Although the posters on this page are very different from one another, they all make use of dynamic flat color.

01 Client: Seattle Theatre Group
Design: Invisible Creature

02 Client: Heroes on Canvas/A Blue Chicken
Design: Eelco van den Berg

03 Client: Wolverhampton City Council
Design: Début

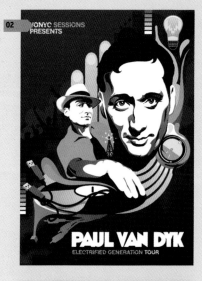

JAZZ NOW

zondag 14 september

De clubgeneratie met een voorliefde voor jazz haalt haar hart op tijdens de nieuwe maandelijkse avond van Off_Corso: 'Jazz Now'.
Van nujazz tot cooljazz, van soul tot funk en van fusion tot experimenteel is Off_Corso elke tweede zondag van de maand hét jazzcentrum van Rotterdam.

Zondag 14 september

Jules Deelder
André Dadi
Barkode

Off_Corso
Kruiskade 22, Rotterdam
tijd: 20.00 - 02.00 uur
prijs: €8,-

www.off-corso.nl

04 Client: Jazznow/Barkode

Design: Eelco van den Berg

Solutions

Project: Promotional posters
Design: Jeff Leak

This set of three posters promotes a live concert, the latest album, and a single by The Varine. Jeff Leak has manipulated full-color photographs of funerary statues to create a moody and powerful backdrop to the distressed typewriter font used for the main headings. The darkness in the character of the images, as well as the heavy colors and tones, suggests rather dramatic music, possibly with religious overtones, and the style of the type injects a contrasting, informal, more spontaneous nature. This unusual combination of image and type could imply a niche style of music. Supporting text is set at a small size and always aligned vertically on the right; while headings are set at different angles and in varying positions on each poster, they all bleed off at the edges to maintain continuity.

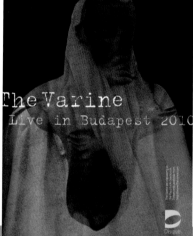

"The designers who do best in the music field are the ones who view their work as visual poetry rather than as a solution provider. This is a relatively recent shift in the mandate of the graphic designer compared with the modernist point of view by which the designer was a service provider and solution generator."

Peter Crnokrak, The Luxury of Protest

Project: Promotional posters
Design: Bright Pink

This set of posters for fictitious band Urban Arc suggests that their music appeals to a broader audience and age range than the previous set. The lively angular figures, together with the angled headline type and graphics, signifies vibrant music with pace, volume, and aspects of discord. The posters all have individuality, yet retain characteristics of the one design style, and this anchors them in the same promotion.

"The first bit of advice I would give is to really know who you are designing for. I think designs for music often suffer from going after a certain design style rather than trying to capture the essence of the music or the personality of the band. This is difficult to do, but is something I always try to keep in mind."

Jason Munn, The Small Stakes

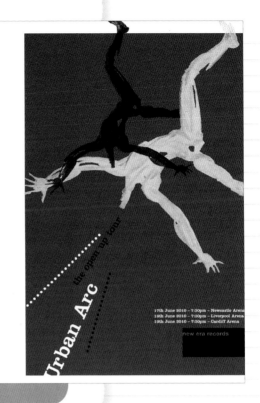

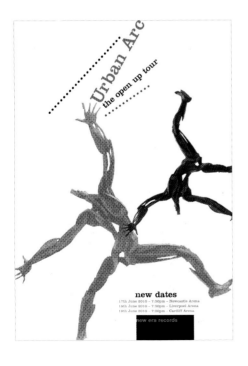

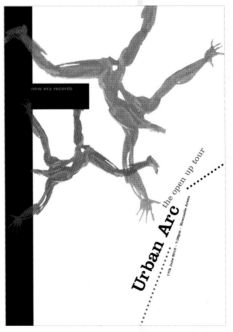

Project: Promotional posters
Design: Howard Read

All five posters in this set for Urban Arc combine distinctive grayscale, hand-rendered illustrations of rather stark urban environments, with strong blocks of color and a clear sans serif typeface. Compositionally, the way the elements build implies that the music of Urban Arc is structured, but the images as a whole also suggest unpredictability. The design approach suggests that the genre belongs to an urban youth "style tribe." As the illustrations and graphic constructs are sufficiently dynamic to attract attention, it is appropriate that only "Urban Arc" is large enough to be read from a distance.

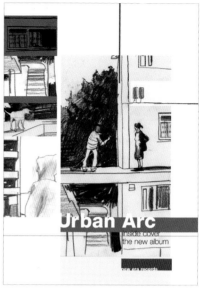

the open up tour

Urban Arc

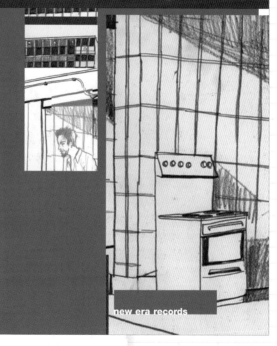

new era records

Urban Arc

the open up tour

12th June 2010 – 7:30pm – Birmingham NIA
13th June 2010 – 7:30pm – Sheffield Arena
14th June 2010 – 7:30pm – Manchester MEN Arena
15th June 2010 – 7:30pm – Glasgow SECC

new era records

Brief 03

CD covers & poster

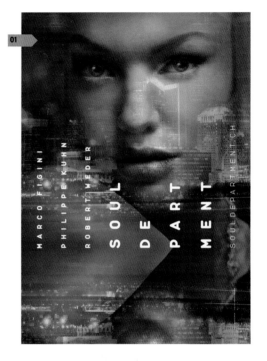

01

The brief

**Design a CD single and album cover, and
a promotional poster for a real or fictitious
artist or band**

The brief explained

Target market

Styling details relating to your chosen artist or band
are certainly going to form an integral part of your
design in trying to appeal to the appropriate target
audience. If the genre you have chosen has any
endemic cultural characteristics, your design must
respond to those. In order to ascertain the target
market of a style of music with which you are not
particularly familiar, observe the audience, listen to
the music, and investigate the origins and influences
of the artist, band, or genre.

Requirements

To originate a design approach that can be applied
to a CD single and album cover, and a poster, as well
as having scope for applications within merchandising
and online promotion. The designs must capture
and visually interpret the style of the artist(s) and
their music, and communicate this to the intended
audience. The covers and poster must encourage
interest in the artist(s) and boost sales of their music.
All of the designs should include the name of the
artist or band, the name of the single or album,
and the logo of the music publisher.

01 Client: Soul Department/Marco Figini
Design: Lorenzo Geiger

02 Client: Soul Department/Marco Figini
Design: Lorenzo Geiger

Methodology

Research

Your research should focus on examples of design for concerts and launches of new albums. In these instances a special "house style" is often created in order to give a recognizable character to all designs related to the concert and/or album. This design style then becomes synonymous not only with a specific artist or group of artists, but also with their work and music at a particular time.

Choose a real or fictitious artist or band. While it may be tempting to design for performers you are familiar with and like, be aware that they could come with a predetermined character and style that is difficult to incorporate in your designs. It may be more beneficial to select a style of music—folk, hip-hop, ambient, or jazz—and make up a fictitious name for the artist or band, as this will enable a completely fresh approach.

Once you've selected the subject matter for the CD single, album, and poster, spend time understanding and appreciating other designs within the same genre. As the type of music will determine the target audience, you should also analyze a wide range of designs focused on that audience in order to ascertain what visual language your target audience "speaks."

Exploration and thumbnails

Listen to the style of music you have chosen. Note its rhythms, volume, pace, and timbre. Certain mark-making materials and implements could help to capture its character: particular colors and relationships of colors may have qualities that can convey the mood or atmosphere you want, and the music may trigger images of people, activities, or landscapes that have value as potential subject matter. There is no doubt that a good starting point for visuals in this instance is to be steeped in the music.

It is essential that you choose the name of the artist or band and the titles of the CDs early on in the design process. Select typefaces and groupings of letterforms and words that reflect at least some of the inherent character of these titles. Image content could also be influenced by names and titles, so if you have chosen to design for a fictitious artist(s), it would be expedient to come up with words that are not only appropriate, but also have visual connotations. Ideally, the sound and style of the music, the name of the artist or band, and the visual language on the CDs and the poster should all be linked and integral to the final designs.

Your roughs and thumbnails should explore a wide variety of concepts, using lots of different media and combinations of media. Purely typographic solutions could be very exciting, especially if the type is used in an illustrative manner; hand-rendered imagery could produce extremely personal and attractive ideas; and photographic images could provide a wealth of options. The challenge of the brief is to produce three designs, for three different items, that look as though they belong to each other, yet still have individuality.

Design development

Position type and image in relation to each other before you set your design frame. This method of working will nurture more interesting and dynamic compositions and will also help to focus your attention on alignments and other systems that bring design elements together. Spatial distribution is a significant part of an identity. If, for example, you place type toward the base of the single cover and bleeding off at the right-hand edge, this will form a distinctive part of the identity, so you must follow the principles of positioning type toward the base (or top) of the composition, to bleed off at the edges, on all other items.

Remember always to apply your ideas to all three items; not only are CDs a very different size from posters, they also perform quite different functions, and the single must have an identity that is distinct from the album. Fonts and typographic styling must maintain consistency despite appearing at varying sizes, but imagery may allow more breadth. For example, different subject matter could be used providing the mark-making and presentation are the same; conversely, the media may change so long as the subject matter remains the same. Consistency with variety is a typical design challenge. Stand back and take an objective look at the items—do they appear too disparate, or are they clearly part of the same set?

Completion

You can present your CD designs as flat computer printouts, or as photographs of your printouts slipped into jewel cases. In either case, for a print portfolio, mount your images on neutral-colored, medium-weight card. Ideally, to have a good contrast in scale, the poster should be printed out at full size and presented on the page opposite the CDs in your portfolio. However, if space is at a premium, a printout of the poster alongside photographic prints of made-up jewel cases would work well. Online presentation can also be a very practical way to display your design solutions, whether as a PDF or as separate digital images. Designs can be uploaded to personal or commercial portfolio sites.

01/02/03/04/05/06/07 Client:
Tooth & Nail Records
Design: Invisible Creature

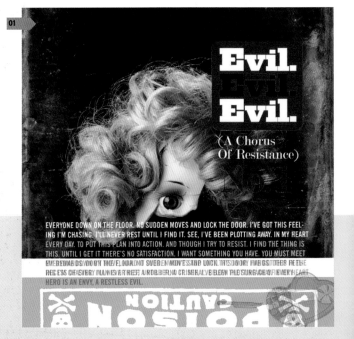

02

05
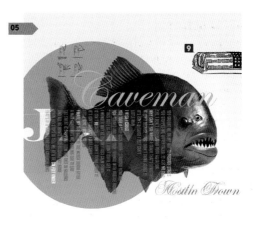

03

06

04

The Forces Of Radio
Have Dropped A Viper
Into The Rhythm Section
Song 3

07

Ensuring that a design approach has sufficient scope to enable varied applications across a number of individual pieces is a common, yet challenging task for the graphic designer. Both of these projects demonstrate themes that have been employed in a number of different ways, maintaining consistency, yet with considerable design diversity.

01 Client: Verona Grove
Design: Madebygregg

01

Charlie Wilhelm: Bass, Vocals. Tony Anders: Vocals, Guitar. Josh Helm: Drums.

Tony Anders: Vocals, Guitar, Piano, Moog
Charlie Wilhelm: Bass, Vocals, Moog
Jason Sutter: Drums, Percussion
Jamie Arentzen: Guitar, Additional Vocals
Lawrence Katz: Additional Guitar on Revolution

The Story

All songs by Tony Anders except Broadcast the News, Everything You Dreamed, No
Words to Say, and Smalltown Celebrity by Tony Anders and Charlie Wilhelm.

Produced By: Jamie Arentzen
Engineered By: Jamie Arentzen, Bruce MacFarlane
Recorded at Pulse Studios, Silver Lake, CA. Courtesy of Butch Walker, and Argyle
Studios, Hollywood, CA, owned by Lawrence Katz.
Additional recording at The Nook, Universal City, CA courtesy of Greg Collins.
Mastered by Bill Dooley at Paramount Recording.
Mixed by Paul Hager at Encore Studios.

Band portrait by Cassie Christenson.
Art direction & design by Gregg Bernstein.

www.myspace.com/veronagrove
www.veronagroveband.com

Thank you: Mom and Dad, Kelly, Ashley, Michelle, Grandpa Ed … for my voice, Grandma Marge,
Grandma Helen, Grandpa John. Mom, Dad, Chris, Carrie, Grandma and Grandpa Dot, Grandma
Cissy, Katrina. Justin Perkins, Pat Magnarella, Tyler Willingham, Nick Fishbaugh, Scott Rosman, Chris
Davies, Sean Mulroney, Jamie Arentzen, Jason Sutter, Bruce MacFarlane, Lawrence Katz, Paul Hager,
Carter Hansen, Tony Zar, Max Harder, Lova, Dave Kaiser (papa K) and Family, The Taylors, DJ, Kos,
Ebz, Will, Ezrah Lockwood and Rock Star Studios, The PRC Interns, Everybody at Mike's Music, Barley
and Hops, Mill Creek, and all other teachers, friends and family that have supported and encouraged
us along the way. Thank You!

Philadelphia Youth Orchestra

Joseph Primavera, Conductor

an american sampler

Philadelphia Youth Orchestra

Joseph Primavera, Conductor

an american sampler

Symphony No. 2	Charles Ives
Salute to George M. Cohan	arr. Aldo Provenzano
An American Sampler	arr. Aldo Provenzano
The Stars and Stripes Forever	John Philip Sousa

Creating an identity for a band or artist and developing, over time, a recognizable visual style across a range of promotional material is a key part of the music industry. Establishing familiar design themes that can be easily identified is integral to ongoing success. The identities on this spread all have the potential to be used and developed as a distinctive visual embodiment of an artist or band.

01 ▶

01 Client: Pearl Jam
Design: Ames Bros

02 Client: various
Design: Lorenzo Geiger

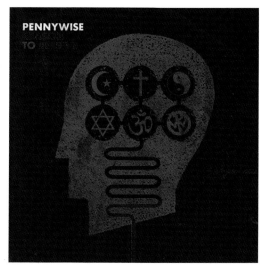

03 Client: My Space Records
Design: Invisible Creature

This diverse, yet coherent use of type, color, style of illustration, texture, and composition is an excellent example of providing an artist with an easily identified, engaging, and individual identity.

04 Client: BEC Recordings
Design: Invisible Creature

Solutions

Project: CD covers and poster
Design: Jeff Leak

Cloudy skies are used to convey a gamut of moods and atmospheres. Here the fluffy white clouds high in a bright blue sky relate to the name of the CD, *Heaven Help*, and the gathering stormy clouds relate to the single *Towards Emotional*. Typographically the design is simple, leaving the imagery to communicate the style of the music, which is likely to appeal to a broad audience.

GmbH towards emotional

"Given a blank canvas to create visuals for a new record, nothing beats the old-fashioned way: live with the music for a few days. Listen to it on constant repeat—in the car, at home, walking around. Listen to it flat on the ground with your eyes closed. Be a teenager about it. Images will come. Then do whatever you can to get the images out of your head in one piece."

Stefan Bucher, 344 Design

Project: CD covers and poster
Design: Jeff Leak

These strange sepia photographs in ornate gilt frames
are extremely arresting. Closer inspection reveals that
the images have been manipulated: there is something
odd about the family groups, and the photos have
a quirky transparency in some sections. Unlike the
previous designs, these are for a style-conscious
market. Note that the typography is integrated into
the image, as though painted onto the gold frames
as for exhibits in an art gallery, and this emphasizes
the precious nature of the music.

"I love when a band has some similar themes running through their artwork,
or better yet an overall consistency that runs throughout their artwork and
design. This consistency could be anything–a color, or a typeface. Sometimes
using the same designer can lead to this naturally."

Jason Munn, The Small Stakes

Project: CD covers and poster
Design: Jeff Leak

Gothic lettering is the giveaway element of these designs; it has a number of connotations, but in this particular context suggests that the tracks on this album are probably loud and emotive. The distorted and out-of-focus images of open-mouthed faces support this notion because, in red and green on black backgrounds, they are very powerful and a little frightening. The italicized white type reversed through the images and bleeding off at the sides conveys a sense of urgency.

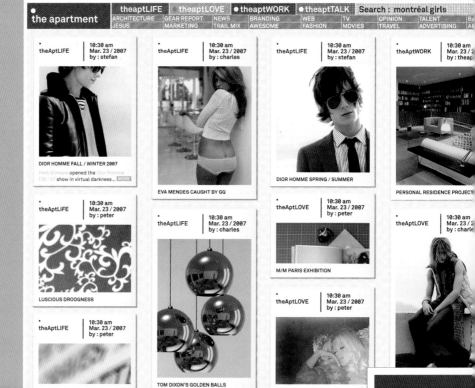

the apartment

theaptLIFE   theaptLOVE   ●theaptWORK   ●theaptTALK   Search : montréal girls

ARCHITECTURE   GEAR REPORT   NEWS   BRANDING   WEB   TV   OPINION   TALENT   BA
JESUS   MARKETING   TRAIL MIX   AWESOME   FASHION   MOVIES   TRAVEL   ADVERTISING   A

theAptLIFE   10:30 am   Mar. 23 / 2007   by : stefan

DIOR HOMME FALL / WINTER 2007

Hedi Slimane opened the Dior Homme FW / 07 show in virtual darkness... MORE

theAptLIFE   10:30 am   Mar. 23 / 2007   by : charles

EVA MENDES CAUGHT BY GQ

theAptLIFE   10:30 am   Mar. 23 / 2007   by : stefan

DIOR HOMME SPRING / SUMMER

theAptWORK   10:30 am   Mar. 23 / 2007   by : theap

PERSONAL RESIDENCE PROJECT

theAptLIFE   10:30 am   Mar. 23 / 2007   by : peter

LUSCIOUS DROOGNESS

theAptLIFE   10:30 am   Mar. 23 / 2007   by : charles

TOM DIXON'S GOLDEN BALLS

theAptLOVE   10:30 am   Mar. 23 / 2007   by : peter

M/M PARIS EXHIBITION

theAptLOVE   10:30 am   Mar. 23 / 2007   by : charle

theAptLIFE   10:30 am   Mar. 23 / 2007   by : peter

WALKER ART CENTRE IDENT

theAptLOVE   10:30 am   Mar. 23 / 2007   by : peter

AGENT PROVACATEUR

M

Home
News
Compositions
Publications
Biography
Contact Miguel

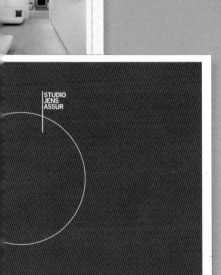

Section 05
Screen-based design

For the novice, taking a leap into the technical world of web design can be a daunting and agonizing experience, but there are plenty of inspiring, confidence-building resources, including books, magazines, and websites, that can help with this transition. These three projects will build your confidence and increase your expertise.

The conceptual and aesthetic aspects of screen-based design are similar to those of print-based design, but the structural and hierarchical challenges of designing a website are very different. However, dealing with this should not be beyond an experienced website user. Jeff Leak of boing! describes this difference as "challenging the designer to work in a nonlinear manner as the viewer of a website should, in theory, be able to access any area of a site at any point. Design for print projects requires the designer to create effective linear hierarchical structures, such as the page-by-page format of a magazine or brochure."

Getting to grips with the hierarchy of your website can be complicated. Start by working through and understanding the content so that you can give careful consideration to a logical sequencing for your site design. Providing the user with a successful, easy-to-understand site navigation system is of vital importance, and drawing out a site plan in thumbnail form is a good way of ironing out any potential difficulties. Consider focusing on the main sections of your proposed site to begin, then work through the secondary and tertiary navigational needs. Ask yourself questions such as, "How many pages will the planned site include?" and "What type of pages will be most suitable?" Remember that presenting your audience with an organized, logical structure will make your website easier to use.

01 Client: The Museum of Modern Art
Design: RenderMonkey Design

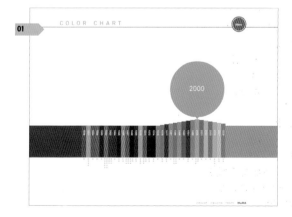

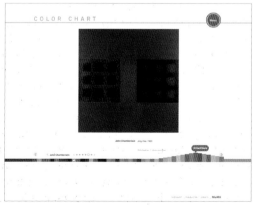

Consider how your decisions will affect the accessibility
of the site right from the start of the design process.
A site built using HTML-authoring software will be the most
universally accessible, but there are alternatives. Sites designed
using Flash offer the tantalizing possibility of movement, more
typographic flexibility, and greater compositional diversity, but
this will probably reduce the number of people able to access
the site. Typographic decisions, fundamental to accessibility
and legibility, are more restricted for screen-based designs
than for print. Gregory Paone of Paone Design Associates offers
this advice. "Typeface selection is one of the greatest challenges
designers face with respect to digital applications. However,
with more fonts becoming available specifically for screen
use, and hardware technology refining resolution, the task
is less daunting than it was 10 years ago. Still, designers must
understand that the number of variables beyond their control
is great, when the myriad of monitors connected to the world
wide web are considered."

Paone continues, "Simplicity of design is paramount.
Typefaces based on a classical form, whether rendered in
a traditional or a contemporary style, generally provide greater
readability. Open letterforms with larger x-heights and proper
spacing (kerning and leading) tend to work best. Overly ornate
styles (especially script fonts) and condensed fonts, when
compounded by poor choices in size and color, will ultimately
defeat legibility. Testing typefaces on multiple platforms and
applications is a critical exercise which should be employed
in the earliest stages of the design development."

Jeff Leak of boing! offers other interesting advice
concerning accessibility. "I would recommend to anyone
interested in learning more about design for screen, that they
look at the Web Accessibility Initiative (http://www.w3.org/WAI/)
as this site offers a considerable amount of fascinating insight
into accessibility in general. I have found it invaluable."

02 Client: 344
Design
Design: 344 Design

03 Client: Save the
Children
Design: Applied Works

Glossary

accessibility this refers to how usable a website is to how many people; the aim is to give equal access to information and functionality to as many people as possible

CSS abbreviation for cascading style sheets; this system allows authors and readers to attach a specific style, for such things as fonts, colors, and spacing, to HTML

GIF abbreviation for graphic interchange format, a format for pictures transmitted pixel by pixel over the Internet

HTML abbreviation for hypertext markup language, a computer language used to create web documents that include text, image, sound, video, and hyperlinks

HTTP abbreviation for hypertext transfer protocol, a computer protocol for transferring information across the Internet

hypertext text that is coded to provide readers with a link to another "page" on the Internet

image optimization the preparation of an image for use on the web; this involves reducing the file size by lowering the resolution to 72dpi and restricting the number of colors

ISP abbreviation for Internet service provider, the party providing a connection to the Internet. Some users have a cable or wireless link to their ISP, while others dial an ISP by phone; they send and receive information over the phone line and the ISP then forwards the information over the Internet

JAVA a computer programming language

JPEG abbreviation for Joint Photographic Experts Group, this is a computer file format for the compression and storage of digital image files

kerning inter-character spacing in typography

navigation system a series of clear routes and links that take visitors to different areas of a website

pixel (picture element) the smallest unit of information in a digital image

PNG abbreviation for Portable Network Graphics, this is a computer file format for the compression and storage of digital image files

resolution a measure of the sharpness or amount of detail held within a digital image file

RGB abbreviation for red, green, blue, the three primary colors of light, used to create all colors on a computer screen

RSS this abbreviation may refer to one of three specifications: Rich Site Summary (RSS 0.91); RDF Site Summary (RSS 0.9, 1.0 and 1.1); or the most commonly known, Really Simple Syndication (RSS 2.0). It describes a method for collecting, publishing, and editing web resources from periodically updated websites

SEO abbreviation for search engine optimization; this is the process of improving the volume or quality of traffic to a website from search engines

splash page an initial website page used to capture the user's attention for a short time as a promotion or lead-in to the site

URI abbreviation for Uniform Resource Identifier, the term for all types of names and addresses that refer to objects on the web

URL abbreviation for Uniform Resource Locator, the unique address of an object on the Internet

Web-authoring software computer programs used to produce a functioning website

WYSIWYG abbreviation for "what you see is what you get;" a WYSIWYG computer application is one that enables you to see on the display screen exactly what will appear when the document is printed or displayed on the web

Reading list

**About Face 3: The Essentials
of Interaction Design**
Alan Cooper, Robert Reimann, David Cronin

Airside
Airside

**Communicating Design: Developing
Web Site Documentation for
Design and Planning**
Dan Brown

**Design for New Media: Interaction
Design for Multimedia and the Web**
Lon Barfield

Designing Interactions
Bill Moggridge

**Left to Right: The Cultural Shift
from Words to Pictures**
David Crow

**Motion Blur 2: Multidimensional
Moving Imagemakers (v. 2)**
onedotzero

Motion by Design
Spencer Drate

**MTIV Process, Inspiration,
and Practice for the New
Media Designer**
Hillman Curtis

Type in Motion
Matt Woolman and J. Bellantoni

Understanding Animation
Paul Wells

**Visible Signs: An Introduction
to Semiotics**
David Crow

Websites
Cube Collection

Equipment

- Marker paper
- Pencils
- Markers/colored pencils
- Ruler/set square
- Typeface reference
- Screen-based (RGB) color-matching
  reference
- Computer with internet access
- HTML authoring software
- Quality image-manipulation software

Brief 01

● ○ ○

Home page & navigation system

The brief

Design a home page and navigation system for a fictitious website

The brief explained

Target market
Select the most appropriate target audience for your chosen home page. This involves careful analysis and consideration of the age range, gender, and lifestyle of the audience. For example, if the character of the selected product, service, or organization promoted by the new home page appeals specifically to an audience with distinctive lifestyle characteristics, the home page should reflect these in order to communicate effectively. It can be helpful to define other products or pastimes that your intended audience would favor in order to build up an accurate picture of the website's potential visitors.

Requirements
To produce a concept for a home page with an effective and interesting navigation system that enables visitors to get a quick understanding of how to maneuver around the finished site. Your designs should include every element and detail that an audience would need to establish realistic and beneficial interaction. While this page must be produced digitally, it does not need to be linked to a complete site. The page must be 600 x 800 pixels.

01 Client: KBNK
Design: Brighten The Corners

01

02 Client: FACT (Friends of Alternative and
Complementary Therapies Society)
Design: Splash Interactive

03 Client: The Green Party of the United States
Design: Abigail Smith

Methodology

Research

For this project you will need to select an organization
or company to publicize. If you choose one that is
familiar to you, you may not need to spend much
time studying the style, character, occupation, and
objectives of the company. However, if you choose
a company that you don't know, you will need to
devote some time to becoming familiar with it.
As well as reading any available articles in magazines
and brochures or on the Internet, it might be possible
for you to visit the company, and experience the
workings of the selected group firsthand.

You could divide your research for this project
into two strands: gathering detail on the company
and its identity; and observing the home pages, site
structures, and navigation systems of other sites.
Be careful to judge these sites critically and take
note of both poor- and good-quality design, as this
will help you recognize what to avoid and what to
take into consideration.

Analyze the main focus of the home page to
ensure that it will be accessible for the intended
audience. Research appropriate fonts, colors,

relationships of scale, and use of imagery. It is likely
that these will be established if the organization you
select already has a successful visual identity.

Make sure you know what the website needs to
communicate as a whole—this will help you develop
the most effective form of navigation. Working out
how details link and how they can be easily accessed
at any point during the experience of using a website
is a vital element of the research and planning
process of web design and demands an excellent
appreciation of not only the subject matter of the
site, but also the audience.

Exploration and thumbnails

Inevitably designers jot down notes and explore
options on layout paper as part of their background
research. Although your solution to this brief will be
viewed for the most part on-screen, it is a good idea
to develop ideas and thumbnails on paper first: this
will allow you to make the most of design options
that might otherwise be limited by your technical
know-how. Of course, there are screen-based options
that are difficult to visualize on paper, including
actions that cause or relate to movement, but careful
annotation can help you with this.

This project provides just an introduction to
screen-based design, so you will not be faced with
many of the time-consuming dilemmas that would
arise during the development of a complete website.
However, in order for this short brief to be of value,
you must keep the "bigger picture" in mind.

Remember to design within the correct proportion for screen use as you work through thumbnail designs. Home pages need to be 600 x 800 pixels to ensure that every area of the finished design will be visible on-screen.

Design development

Having done your research you should have a clear idea about what information you need to include on the home page; working up visuals will give you the opportunity to experiment with alternative ways of bringing detail together. As with many graphics projects, a grid structure is an extremely useful and effective system that will not only help you bring together and organize all the elements on your home page, but also set a template for all subsequent pages.

When working on roughs for screen projects, you must consider a number of technical facts. Unlike design for print, for which it is possible to create almost any color, when you design for the web you are restricted to 256 RGB colors. Rather than viewing this as a limitation, grasp it as an exciting design challenge.

Consider the positioning of navigation links. Make sure they are clearly defined, easy to spot, and simple to use. Always keep in mind that different audiences will be using different computers and different browsing software. Make sure all of these potential viewers will be able to have a useful experience when viewing this home page; be sure that nothing will be obscured or illegible. Once you are happy with your roughs, try them out using web-authoring software. This gives you the chance to sample the home-page design in a variety of browsers. Some of the examples in the reference section use a number of different programs, but as accessibility is a vital consideration for any web designer, the only way to be confident that almost any audience can "read" the detail and information in a design is to produce an HTML site. This format will undoubtedly limit the number of typefaces it is possible to use, as only a small percentage of faces is available on any one computer; if a font is not found, a default will be substituted by the computer software and this could result in changes to line

breaks and a dramatically different appearance. However, careful design consideration can produce some exciting, effective, and appealing results.

The design development stage also involves preparation of imagery, including image optimization to ensure that photographs or illustrations load speedily. Remember that, unlike designing for print, all digital images must be 72dpi: lower than this will result in poor quality and higher would be ineffectual, as monitors only show images at 72dpi. Discuss your final designs with friends and colleagues—an impartial second opinion can be very helpful.

Completion

Having settled on a design approach and solution and resolved any issues flagged up by your screen-based tests, your design will be complete and ready for display in a digital portfolio. It is also possible to feature printouts from screen shots of the home page in a print portfolio, which ensures the design can be viewed even when no computer is available.

01 Client: Spiritualized
Design: Applied Works

Rolling over design elements in the web pages on this spread has the effect of activating and identifying links to other areas of the various sites; for example, rolling over the top hat on the Holy Mountain website opens up the link to the About Us page, rolling over the pink concentric circles shows hidden links to a variety of pages within the 344 Design site, and hovering over the colored bars in the Armando Reverón website gives access to different periods of work.

02 Client: Boz Temple-Morris
Design: Brighten the Corners

03 Client: 344 Design
Design: 344 Design

04 Client: Hemming Morse
Design: Vrontikis Design Office

02

03

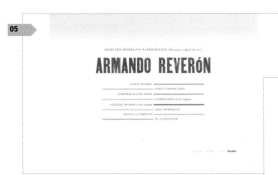

04

05

05 Client: The Museum of Modern Art
Design: RenderMonkey Design

These websites, all very different from each other, show that navigational links can be set in straightforward typographic listings or in illustrations and photographs. Whatever you choose, make sure that the linking "vehicle" is appropriate for the topic and the audience.

01 Client: Universal Music

Design: Holler

01

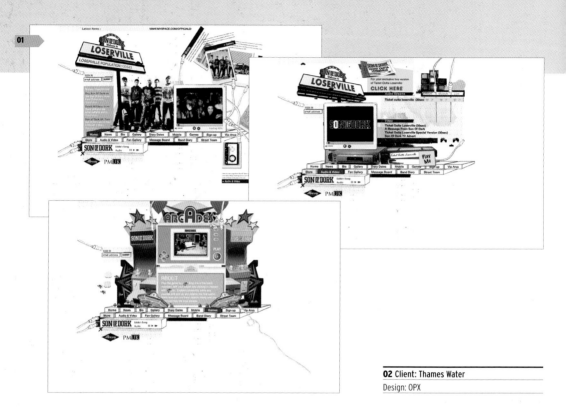

02 Client: Thames Water

Design: OPX

02

Environment: Part of an ongoing body of work focusing on the idiosyncratic beauty of found natural objects, these images were used for a series of posters and publications produced for the US-based charity Rainforest Action Network (RAN); a collaboration with Matt Willey of Studio8 Design. Further work on the theme includes a series of prints considering the conflict between environment and urban, industrial development.

PROFILE

GILES REVELL
PORTFOLIO ENVIRONMENT

PROFILE

03

03 Client: Giles Revell
Design: Studio8 Design

NEXT STEP FORWARD

AECOM

GRADUATE CAREER OPPORTUNITIES

Welcome

Want to build a better world? Keen to work with people who are committed to a sustainable future? At AECOM, our goal is to enhance and sustain the built, natural and social environment. That means planning and designing the cities, the buildings, the transport systems and the infrastructure that countries need to sustain economic and social growth. It also means protecting the natural environment for future generations. It's a big challenge.

If this challenge excites you, step this way.

Click on the shoes to see our stories

Name
Gemma Clarke
Job Title
Structural Engineer
Location
London, UK

Name
Wilson Man
Job Title
Graduate Engineer
Location
Hong Kong, China

Name
Patricia Fonseca
Job Title
Landscape Designer
Location
San Francisco, USA

Please scroll right

04

WORKING WITH US
Our stories
About AECOM
Sustainability & community
Our approach & opportunities
Letter from CEO

OUR WORK
Architecture & Planning
Building Engineering
Energy & Power
Environment
International Development
Program Management
Transportation
Water

CONTACT US
Choose where you are:
USA
Canada
UK & Europe
Middle East & North Africa
Australasia
Hong Kong, China & Asia

APPLY NOW!

NEXT STEP FORWARD

AECOM

GRADUATE CAREER OPPORTUNITIES

Name
Patricia Fonseca
Job Title
Landscape Designer
Location
San Francisco, USA

Name
Nikki Duncan
Job Title
Staff Consultant
Location
Washington DC, USA

Name
Sophie Potvin-Champagne
Job Title
Junior Electrical Engineer
Location
Montreal, Canada

Name
Phil Thompson
Job Title
Junior Structural Engineer
Location
New York, USA

Name
Mark Barnett
Job Title
Environmental

<<   >>

WORKING WITH US
Our stories
About AECOM
Sustainability & community
Our approach & opportunities
Letter from CEO

OUR WORK
Architecture & Planning
Building Engineering
Energy & Power
Environment
International Development
Program Management
Transportation
Water

CONTACT US
Choose where you are:
USA
Canada
UK & Europe
Middle East & North Africa
Australasia
Hong Kong, China & Asia

APPLY NOW!

04 Client: AECOM
Design: OPX

NEXT STEP FORWARD

AECOM

GRADUATE CAREER OPPORTUNITIES

NIKKI DUNCAN
INTERNATIONAL DEVELOPMENT

Watch Q&A Video   Gallery

Name
Nikki Duncan
Job Title
Staff Consultant
Location
Washington DC, USA

Download profile PDF

View other stories:
Gemma Clarke / Wilson Man / Patricia Fonseca / Sophie Potvin-Champagne / Phil Thompson / Mark Barnett / Ahmed Daly

WORKING WITH US
Our stories
About AECOM
Sustainability & community
Our approach & opportunities
Letter from CEO

OUR WORK
Architecture & Planning
Building Engineering
Energy & Power
Environment
International Development
Program Management
Transportation
Water

CONTACT US
Choose where you are:
USA
Canada
UK & Europe
Middle East & North Africa
Australasia
Hong Kong, China & Asia

APPLY NOW!

01 Client: The Museum of Modern Art

Design: RenderMonkey Design

Color Chart is an online gallery of artists' work from 1950 to the present. As it features work that focuses on color, the opening page shows vibrant rotating circles reversed through a vivid cyan background. A bright pink button invites you to "view artist" and you are given the option of viewing work by timeline, by medium, or by artist. It is very clear to the user how to progress through the site, and the simple animation and exciting color relationships make the process both interesting and compelling. For example, if you are viewing work "by artist," as your cursor rolls over the artists' names, the colored bars rise up; when you pause over one bar, a circle in a corresponding color pops up and as you click on that circle, examples of work by the selected artist appear. Click on a specific piece and a larger image is displayed along with basic information about that image. Moving forward or backward within this site is straightforward, yet visually appealing. It is an excellent example of a site with a pleasing function and aesthetic.

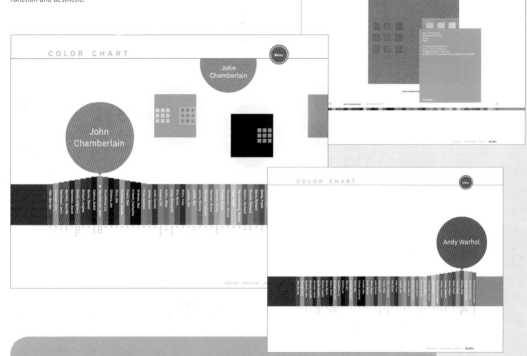

"The axiom 'less is more,' from a communication point of view, is simply absurd. Complexity communicates volumes when used in the proper context, and conversely, so does minimalism. A careful reading of the state of visual culture is the skill talented designers posses that allows them to determine which is the more appropriate path to take: the complex or the simple one."

Peter Crnokrak, The Luxury of Protest

02 Client: Lulu Sturdy

Design: Rebecca Foster Design

An extremely striking and space-rich page, with nine short strips of very unusual colors grouped in the top left corner, establishes the Ndali Vanilla website. Click "enter" and these colors lengthen to the full page depth, with various headings running vertically along each. You can then click on any strip and it travels out to the right of the page to reveal the relevant text and images for that section; click on another color and the existing bar moves back to the left to be replaced by the newly selected one. This website contains a lot of copy, but the simple and engaging navigation system encourages you to look through every page. The copy is broken down into different textures, tones, and colors to help make it more interesting and "digestible," and the grid structure leads you from column to column.

02

enter
site requires
flash player plugin
1024 x 768
6.7 million colours

ndali vanilla

01 Client: Ames Bros

Design: Ames Bros

Ames Bros has a very distinctive style of design and illustration and has used this, together with quirky animations of a 3D viewer, to take you through their work and website. Click on a topic in the bar at the top of a page and the 3D viewer will be loaded with the appropriate disc; after a brief pause the red "wind on" indicates that it is active and, as you click on it, the images alongside change to display examples of work. Generally speaking, Ames Bros work is retro, so the use of the 3D viewer is appropriate, and also provides a fascinating vehicle to showcase the brothers' portfolio.

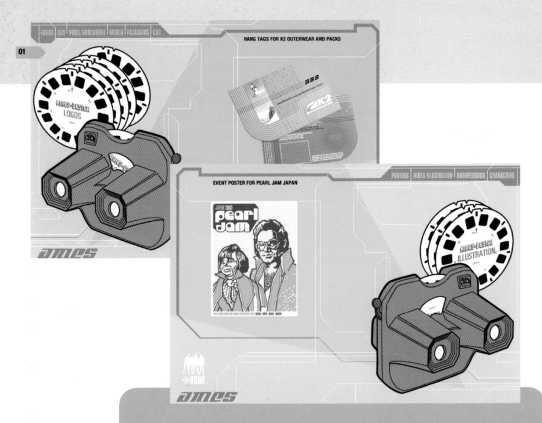

"I don't enjoy design trickery or showboating for its own ends. How many times do you have to sit through a flashy animation just to get to your reason for visiting the site before it gets tiresome? I guess that I'm still an advocate of design being a tool for good, for improving accessibility and functionality, but without forgetting user enjoyment."

Jeff Leak, boing!

02 Client: Miguel Mera

Design: Applied Works

Miguel Mera is a composer for film and television, and his website uses a clear grid system to place text and image in familiar and consistently recurring spaces. The landing page heralds the format by establishing a capital "M" and list of sections in the top left corner, and these remain in the same positions throughout. The initial "M" is located and color coded to draw you to the starting point of each page and simple columns of text, set in luxurious amounts of white space, reassure you that you will be able to find everything you need. Sound bars enable the playing of music tracks, both in isolation and with films or programs.

Solutions

Project: Home page and navigation system
Design: Bright Pink

The Lapley Little Theatre website offers a great deal of information, skillfully managed through a very efficient navigation system. The home page presents a wide selection of "click-on" links to different pages within the website, while a consistent band across the top enables access to new pages with a link to return to the home page at any point; it also gives you the opportunity to locate or contact the theatre whenever you may choose. It is important that users can find new information in a site easily, and it is equally important that they can backtrack to pages they have already viewed; this proposed navigation system satisfies both these needs.

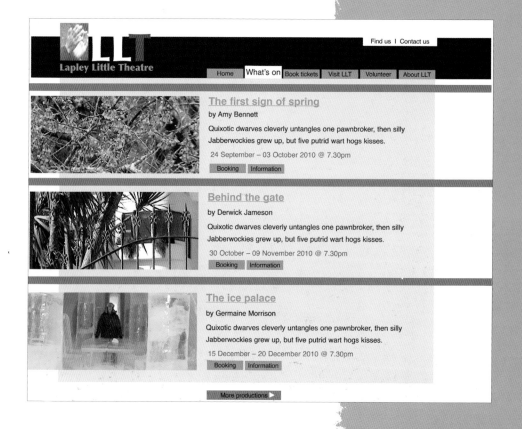

Project: Home page and navigation system
Design: Bright Pink

Toys are fun and the Toytown navigation system attempts to capture some of the playfulness of the products it sells. The home page provides you with very little typography—merely a row of brightly colored geometric shapes along its base. As you roll over each one it enlarges, displaying the name of a category of toys and throwing up a fan of shapes which list different sections in that category; you then click onto whichever section you wish to view. This same "rollover" and "click-on" process is available at the base of each page, enabling the user to move forward or backward to any page, at any time.

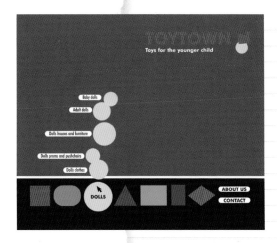

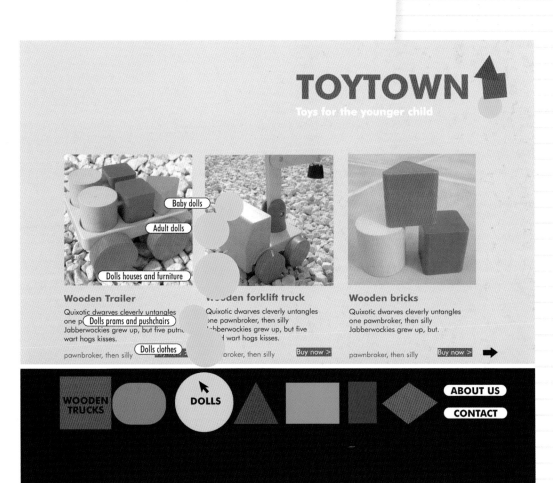

Brief 02

E-card

The brief

Design an e-card that promotes healthy eating

The brief explained

Target market

This project aims to encourage young adults to eat healthily. In order to communicate effectively, the visual language of the design needs to incorporate the styles, colors, fashions, and language that will appeal to this specific audience. The target market is likely to be living at home, but taking an increasing interest in being independent.

Requirements

The e-card must be lively and informative, and must communicate with the target audience in a casual manner. Solutions do not have to be animated. The card should be 400 x 300 pixels. Concepts can involve a mix of image and text and must educate readers and encourage them to eat a better diet and enjoy a healthier lifestyle.

01 Client: Fairwinds Press
Cover design: Mary Ann Smith
Page design: Leslie Haimes

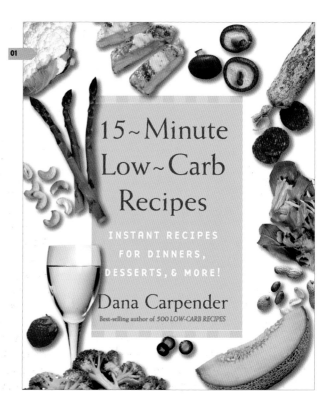

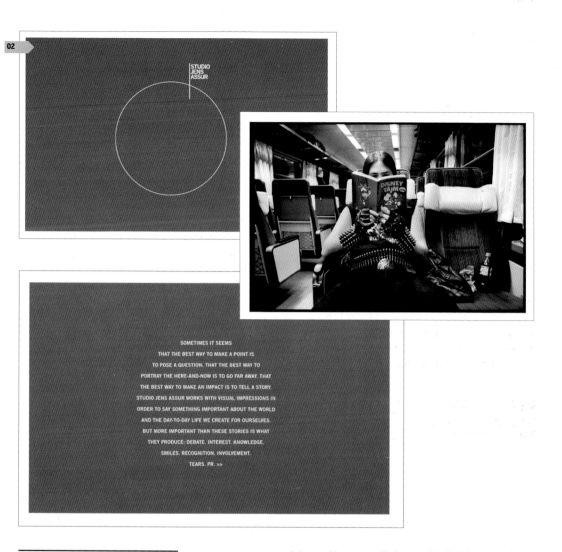

SOMETIMES IT SEEMS
THAT THE BEST WAY TO MAKE A POINT IS
TO POSE A QUESTION. THAT THE BEST WAY TO
PORTRAY THE HERE-AND-NOW IS TO GO FAR AWAY. THAT
THE BEST WAY TO MAKE AN IMPACT IS TO TELL A STORY.
STUDIO JENS ASSUR WORKS WITH VISUAL IMPRESSIONS IN
ORDER TO SAY SOMETHING IMPORTANT ABOUT THE WORLD
AND THE DAY-TO-DAY LIFE WE CREATE FOR OURSELVES.
BUT MORE IMPORTANT THAN THESE STORIES IS WHAT
THEY PRODUCE: DEBATE. INTEREST. KNOWLEDGE.
SMILES. RECOGNITION. INVOLVEMENT.
TEARS. PR. >>

02 Client: Studio Jens Assur
Design: BankerWessel

Methodology
Research

You will need to investigate the target audience for this project to make sure you understand the young adult market, its eating habits, its attitude to food in general, and what priority it affords a healthy lifestyle. To produce an e-card that will encourage this group to pursue healthy eating habits you will need to spend time becoming familiar with the visual styles and language that appeal to it. It is never wise to assume that if you are part of a target market you will automatically have a clear knowledge and understanding of it. Look at a selection of e-card designs and spend time searching for examples of effective use of the Internet to convey campaigning messages—messages that improve lives, change attitudes, and alter behavior.

An e-card is very similar to a conventional postcard or greetings card although, being digital, it could be described as more environmentally friendly. An e-card can often be personalized to address a recipient by name, or to provide a distinctive personal message.

Exploration and thumbnails

After spending time researching and making notes on your initial thoughts, you are ready to start exploring and developing your design concepts. On a practical note, this brief specifies a precise size—400 x 300 pixels. It is vital that you keep this in mind and produce all your visuals in direct proportion to this final size. Color use for this project is restricted to the 256 RGB colors that can be viewed on-screen, so select them from a screen-based chart. Remember that you are designing an e-card, not a website: you need to get your message across quickly, so avoid too many linked pages.

Consider not only the aesthetics that will appeal to a style-conscious young audience, but also the message itself. What kind of language would be effective; how should you speak to this group? There is no point including a recipe if your audience isn't interested in cooking.

In the course of your research you will have come across marketing techniques such as celebrity endorsements and seen advertisements that use music as a mnemonic device: it is worth exploring such options in your thumbnails and roughs.

Design development

Once you have explored your design options on layout paper, you need to assess their viability on-screen. Do not simply select the design you think seems the best and develop just this one approach: you could miss out on surprising alternatives that prove to be more effective. The process of design is all about working through alternatives and not simply producing one solution in isolation. It is also worth considering the use of alternative vocabulary to see if it is possible to enhance communication. Ask other people for their opinion. Explain the aims and objectives of the brief and, if possible, find individuals who fit the demographic category this e-card is intended to reach.

01 Client: Fairwinds Press
Design: Laura McFadden Design
Page design: Leslie Haimes

01

Carrots

What's the very first thing you think of if someone uses the term "health food"? For many people, it's carrots. Well-known naturopath Dr. Michael Murray calls carrots "the king of the vegetables," and for good reason. Recent human studies have indicated that as little as one carrot a day could possibly cut the rate of lung cancer in half.

That's not to say you should smoke and eat carrots. But it is to say that the cancer-fighting properties of this great vegetable should be taken seriously. Carrots are high in *carotenoids*, antioxidant compounds found in plants that are associated with a wide range of health benefits. You've probably heard good things about beta-carotene, but that's only one of about 500 members of the carotenoid family. Some research suggests that other carotenoids may be even more important. High carotenoid intake has been associated with a decrease of up to 50 percent in bladder, cervix, prostate, colon, larynx, and esophageal cancer, as well as up to a 20 percent decrease in post-menopausal breast cancer. Carrots are also high in *alpha-carotene*, another carotenoid that appears to have health benefits of its own. In fact, one report published in *NCI Cancer Weekly* by Michiaki Murakoshi, who led a team of biochemists at Japan's Kyoto Prefectural University of Medicine, contends that alpha-carotene may be more powerful than beta-carotene in inhibiting processes that may lead to tumor growth.

Although one badly designed study a few years ago seemed to indicate that beta-carotene by itself had no value in preventing cancer, what wasn't well publicized is that the study subjects were heavy smokers and that the beta-carotene given to them was a synthetic kind that behaves quite differently in the body than the real deal. The real lesson from that study is that the carotenoids perform best working as a unit, and should be obtained in their natural—not synthetic —form. According to Walt Willett, Ph.D., chairman of the department of nutrition at the Harvard School of Public Health, dozens of studies show beneficial associations between eating fruits and vegetables high in carotenoids and less cardiovascular disease, not to mention less prostate, lung, stomach, colon, breast, cervix, and pancreatic cancer.

Why Your Mom Was Right about Carrots

Put carrots in the column labeled "things mother was right about after all." Carrots really are good for your eyes. They're a great source of lutein and zeaxanthin, two other carotenoids that, when working together, have shown enormous promise in protecting the eyes and helping to prevent macular degeneration and cataracts. Both alpha-carotene and beta-carotene convert in the body to vitamin A, which, in addition to being a great antioxidant and immune system stimulator, turbocharges the formation of a purple pigment in the eye called *rhodopsin*. Rhodopsin is needed by the eye to see in dim light—it actually raises the effectiveness of the light-sensitive area of the retina—so not getting enough vitamin A can actually lead to night blindness.

Three medium carrots contain 60 mg of calcium, 586 mg of potassium, a little bit of magnesium, phosphorus, and vitamin C, and of course, a whopping 30,000 IUs of vitamin A, including 15,000 units of beta-carotene and 6,000 of alpha-carotene. They also have 5 g of fiber.

Cooked Carrots Prevail

Cooking slightly changes the nutritional content and makes some of the nutrients more bioavailable. But both raw and cooked carrots are healthy.

To get the most out of the carotenoids found in carrots, eat them with a little fat. The carotenoids and vitamin A are fat-soluble nutrients and are better absorbed that way.

Finally, carrots are a favorite ingredient for juicing, and carrot juice is often used as part of a detoxification program. Just be aware that when you juice carrots you're using a lot of them, plus you're removing the fiber, both of which increase the concentration of sugar. That doesn't mean it's not a fantastically healthy juice ingredient, just something you should be aware of if you're sensitive to blood sugar fluctuations. (Juicing carrots with some really low-sugar vegetables like spinach and broccoli lessens the impact.)

WORTH KNOWING

Carrots got a really bad and totally undeserved rap by the low-carb folks because of their high glycemic index. Actually, the glycemic index isn't very important—the glycemic *load* is. The glycemic index tests are done on a 50-g portion of carbohydrate, whereas the load tests are done on real-life portions. A carrot has only about 4 g of carbohydrate, so its glycemic load—the only number that matters—is ridiculously low (about 3 on a scale of 0-40+). You'd have to eat a ton of carrots to get a significant rise in blood sugar. Even so, some very careful diabetes doctors whose opinion I respect still tell patients to beware. For everyone else, I think carrots are absolutely fine.

VEGETABLES

JULY

1

Oh Canada! It must be good to be free . . . sort of. Canada celebrates the establishment of its federal government on July 1st. Now known as Canada Day, it previously was known as Dominion Day and Confederation Day. The day commemorates the British North America Act of July 1, 1867, which gave Canadians home rule. But seeing as it's still a part of the Commonwealth and under the rule of the Queen, we think that, instead of "independence," it's really more like being left to watch the house while Mom runs out to do her errands. Break free, Canada, and have a cocktail!

CANADA COCKTAIL

1½ oz Canadian whisky
½ oz orange liqueur
3 drops bitters
1 sprig mint

Combine all the liquid ingredients over ice in an old-fashioned glass and garnish with a sprig of mint. Easy, eh?

2

The normally soft-spoken and well-behaved Alabama-born and -raised actress Polly Holliday hit it big on '70s TV as the brash, uninhibited, gum-smacking waitress Florence Jean Castleberry (better known as "Flo") on the popular sitcom *Alice*. It's hard to find anybody who grew up in the time of *Alice* who doesn't remember the larger-than-life Flo. Weekly, we were thrilled by the abuse she heaped on her boss, Mel, and sat riveted on the edge of our seats waiting for her signature one-liner that sooner or later always came: "Mel, kiss my grits!" Classic.

KISS MY GRITS

½ oz orange juice
¼ oz lemon juice
1½ oz sloe gin
1 tsp powdered sugar
1 splash of club soda
1 lime wedge

Combine all the ingredients except the club soda and lime wedge in a shaker with ice and shake well. Pour into a Collins glass filled with ice and top off with club soda. Stir well. Garnish with the lime and serve with a bowl of grits.

198

14 Today is the day we celebrate France's independence. It's Bastille Day! As you mix up the tasty treat below, ponder all of the wonderful things the French have given the world: French Bread, French Nails, French Braids, French Cuffs, French Kissing, French's Mustard, French Stewart, Dawn French, Samuel French, *The French Connection, The French Lieutenant's Woman*, French Doors, the French Quarter, French Dressing, the French Maid, How the French Stole Christmas . . . Wait a minute—that last one doesn't seem quite right. Oh well, vive la France!

FRENCH REVOLUTION

2 oz brandy
½ oz framboise liqueur
3 oz chilled Champagne

Pour the brandy and liqueur into a mixing glass over ice. Stir well, and strain into a Champagne flute. Add the Champagne, and serve.

"No government could survive without champagne . . . in the throats of our diplomatic people [it] is like oil in the wheels of an engine."

— JOSEPH DARGENT

211

Completion

After choosing which option to follow, spend time completing design detail, making sure that any functionality is trouble-free and easy to use.

When your design is complete, consider how best to display your work. Online CVs and portfolios are an ideal way of showing screen-based solutions. If you have a print-based portfolio, you might also consider making quality printouts from screenshots.

02 Client: Fairwinds Press
Design: Laura McFadden Design

Inspiration can come from a great number of different sources.
These designs come from printed cookbooks, healthy eating
brochures, promotional banners, and MySpace pages.

01 Client: Fairwinds
Press

Cover design: Mary
Ann Smith

Page design: Leslie
Haimes

02 Client: Fairwinds
Press

Cover design: Dutton
& Sherman Design

Page design: Leslie
Haimes

03 Client: Fairwinds
Press

Design: Laura
McFadden Design

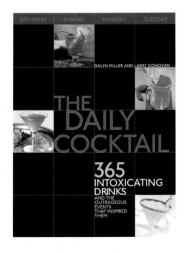

04 Client: Mid-Iowa
Health Foundation
Design: Sayles
Graphic Design

04

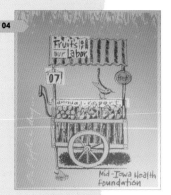

05 Client: Nestlé
Design: Holler

05

OUR JOURNEY BEGINS...

Shreddies

WHICH WE SHARE WITH HASTE

Shreddies

WITH THE MOST INGENIOUS OF THINGS

Shreddies

AS EACH MORNING DESERVES
GOOD. WHOLESOME. TASTE.

Shreddies

06 Client: Channel 4
Design: Holler

06

MEET THE SKINS CREW

COOK

EFFY

Oozing charisma, James Cook pulls off daring acts knowing
Freddie will always be there to bail him out.

VISIT COOK'S PROFILE   VIEW COOK'S VIDEO
VISIT COOK ON E4.COM   ADD COOK TO FRIENDS

Enigmatic and elusive, Effy's the queen bee, attractive to all
around her, utterly in control of herself and totally independent.

VISIT EFFY'S PROFILE   VIEW EFFY'S VIDEO
VISIT EFFY ON E4.COM   ADD EFFY TO FRIENDS

EMILY

NAOMI

Emily Fitch likes being a twin. She's crippled by her own
shyness and depends on her sister to be the dynamic one.

VISIT EMILY'S PROFILE   VIEW EMILY'S VIDEO
VISIT EMILY ON E4.COM   ADD EMILY TO FRIENDS

Naomi Campbell is a beautiful idealist. Passionate, political and
principled, she's the only one who still believe's in anything.

VISIT NAOMI'S PROFILE   VIEW NAOMI'S VIDEO
VISIT NAOMI ON E4.COM   ADD NAOMI TO FRIENDS

Many of the examples here explore ways of making food look appetizing. They give a good overview of the ways in which web pages concerning food and diet present the subject.

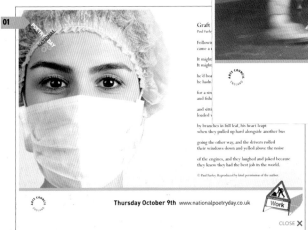

01 Client: National Poetry Day
Design: Broadwave

02 Client: Calistoga Bakery Café
Design: Vrontikis Design Office

03

04

Almond Chocolate Cake

Wine Pairing: Peller Estate Private Reserve Merlot
Yield: 4 servings

Ingredients:

1/2 lb/250g bitter chocolate
1 cup/250ml unsalted butter
1 1/2 cups/375ml icing sugar
1/3 cup/75ml brown sugar
3/4 cup/175ml ground almonds
1/3 cup/75ml all purpose flour
6 eggs, separated

shopping list

1 pkg bitter chocolate
1 unsalted butter
1 bag of icing sugar
1 bag of brown sugar
1 bag of all purpose flour
ground almonds
6 eggs

Preheat oven to 325 F. Grease eight 4-inch springform pans and set aside. Melt the chocolate in a stainless steel bowl over simmering water. Combine the butter and the two sugars in the bowl of a stand mixer and beat at medium speed until pale and thick. Add the egg yolks one at a time until well blended. Add the melted chocolate and mix. Add the almonds and flour and mix to combine thoroughly. Whip 4 egg whites to stiff peaks. Fold into the chocolate batter and mix carefully to combine. Pour the batter into the prepared pans and bake for 35 minutes, or until a toothpick inserted in the middle of the cake comes out clean.

click here to email recipe

main menu   red   white   rosé   recipes   subscribe to Tasting Notes

Kiosk by Splash Interactive

Tel 1-800-220-4321 Email Us   ADD THIS   Locate Nearest Store

...ccessories   News & Events   Wine & Food   Gift Ideas   Contact Us

...Sushi

...Chardonnay

4 sheets nori (dry seaweed)
1 6 ounce canned crab meat, drained
1 avocado - peeled, pitted and sliced

Method:
Combine the water and rice in a saucepan and bring to a boil. Cover, reduce heat to low and simmer for 20 minutes, or until rice is tender and water has been absorbed. Remove from heat and stir in vinegar and pinch of salt. Set aside to cool.
Cover a bamboo sushi mat with plastic wrap to keep the rice from sticking. Place a sheet of seaweed over the plastic. Use your hands to spread the rice evenly onto the sheet, leaving about 1/2 inch of seaweed empty at the bottom.
Arrange crabmeat and avocado across the center of the rice. Lift the mat and roll over the vegetables once and press down. Unroll, then roll again towards the exposed end of the seaweed sheet to make a long roll. You may moisten with a little water to help seal. Set aside and continue with remaining nori sheets, rice and fillings.
Use a sharp wet knife to slice the rolls into 5 or 6 slices. Serve cut side up with your favourite sushi condiments.

keyword search

Trius

PELLER ESTATES

HILLEBRAND

CRÖC CROSSING

Subscribe to Tasting Notes, an eNewsletter from

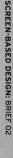

03 Client: Los Angeles Convention
and Visitors Bureau
Design: Vrontikis Design Office

04 Client: Vineyards Estate Wines
Design: Splash Interactive

SCREEN-BASED DESIGN: BRIEF 02

Solutions

Project: E-card
Design: Debbie Ridgway
Debbie Ridgway has used the familiar brown paper bag, associated by many with lunches or take-out meals, so that her designs suggest that the recipes are not only quick, but are also a treat. Prominent arrows take you forward and backward to access information quickly and easily, and the natural color palette and homey typeface work to combine the idea of healthy food with food you will relish.

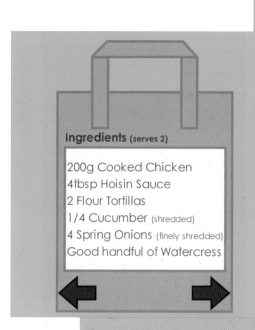

"Simplicity and clarity of presentation should be the designer's goal. The designer should find ways to reduce the information to its barest essence and follow through with an honest and direct design solution that supports the hierarchy."

Gregory Paone, Paone Design Associates

Project: E-card

Design: Jake Stevenson

This uncomplicated, typographic solution aims to tempt young people to eat more healthily. It uses a clear, no-nonsense typeface and a mix of "edible" colors. Only four in the sequence are shown here, but they demonstrate the principle behind Jake Stevenson's design. Following the idea that most people associate healthy food with complicated recipes and long cooking times, he has produced a design that speaks of simplicity and speed through both its visual and verbal language.

Cooking
made
simple

Sea Bass fillets
Ginger, 3 Chillies
3 Garlic Cloves
Soy Sauce

Step 3

When hot, fry the fish in oil
for 5 minutes
skin side down

2x tins fresh tropical fruit
425g can lychees in syrup
2 stems lemongrass
golden caster sugar

Project: E-card
Design: Thomas Pepper

These fresh, "unstyled" photographs, set on a natural wooden surface alongside unsophisticated typography, suggest food that is both wholesome and simple to prepare. Many of the photographs are presented as Polaroids, which sends out the message "quick results." From a design point of view, the choice of font for "meals in minutes" and the mix of systems for image and text groupings could be better considered to make it more cohesive, but there is a sense in which this more amateur aesthetic helps to suggest that eating healthily can be a part of everyone's everyday life.

Project: E-card
Design: Daniel Muir

Daniel Muir has employed a naive, hand-drawn rendering for all his images and text. This picks up on the pleasure and satisfaction of the "handmade," and at the same time reassures that restaurant styling is not required.

A stronger sense of design could have been created by contrasting headings in a formal typeface, using more consistent typographic groupings, and introducing flat areas of color into some of the backgrounds. However, it is always important to understand your target market and this style has the potential to attract attention and communicate well.

"The use of vernacular type or images can create strong associations that affect the overall message of a design. For example, the inclusion of natural materials suggests that a topic is wholesome and environmentally friendly, whereas the appearance of shiny plastics and metals is suggestive of something more stylish and contemporary."

Carolyn Knight and Jessica Glaser, Bright Pink

Brief 03

●●●

Travel website

The brief
**Design a complete website that acts as an
online guide to holiday destinations worldwide**

The brief explained

Target market

This website is aimed at a broad audience with
an age range of 25 to 65; what unites this group is an
enthusiasm for traveling and discovering different
destinations, and the desire to research and plan
a trip before departure. The target market will have
sufficient disposable income for "adventure travel."

The target market is composed of two main groups:
a younger "cash rich, time poor" sector, and an older
group with no dependents.

Requirements

The website concept must include a home page,
navigation system, and sufficient linked web pages
to demonstrate how the site appears and functions.
Designs should include every element of detail
the audience will need to establish realistic and
beneficial interaction. The page should be 600 x 800
pixels, and all pages must have linear connections.

01 Client: Hillebrand Winery
Design: Splash Interactive

01

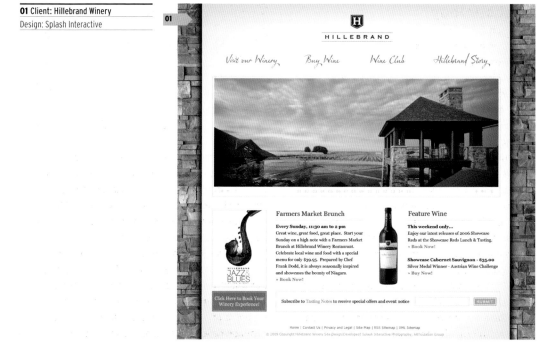

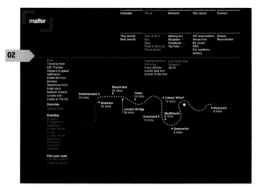

Design: OPX

Design: The Luxury Of Protest

Methodology

Research

This complex and demanding task challenges you to conceive and produce an online environment that will inspire, inform, and capture the interest of viewers. To begin your research, look at other online guides. Take particular note of site plans to see how the audience is intended to progress from page to page. Ask yourself how successful the structure and interactivity of each site is. Do you think it could be improved?

It is also a good idea to look at print-based travel guides. These can provide information about specific locations and cultures and might also suggest what category headings and generic details it would be useful to include. Most print-based travel guides are part of a series and follow a distinct visual identity that copes well with an ever-expanding range of titles. Take time to analyze the scope of these identities, as your travel website should aim to deliver information about diverse locations.

Decide whether your site will have a specific theme, for example, weekend breaks, romantic holidays, cruises, adventure travel in Africa, or educational trips. Make notes about the topics you need to cover, as this will help you select the most effective headings and navigation system.

Look for images that will not only capture the atmosphere of the suggested tour and location, but will also appeal to the intended audience. If you are using photographs, consider whether cropping or rescaling images will enhance the communication of atmosphere and culture.

Exploration and thumbnails

Start bringing your concepts together on paper.
Spend time recording your ideas for a site map
to show how all the separate areas of the site are
connected and make sure that every area is easily
accessible at all times. Think about how best to
create your home page and set the scene for the
subsequent pages of your site. Begin work on a grid
structure that will help you organize the contents of
your finished site and provide design interest, ease
of navigation, and flexibility. Your site will probably
be divided into sections of varying size, length, and
importance—adopting a flexible, yet consistent grid
structure will prove a great help in dealing with this
hierarchical complexity.

Develop your thumbnail ideas across a number
of pages. Spend time considering and originating
a visual treatment for the navigation system and look
at the formulation of a meaningful color palette that
will provide lots of scope for shifts in color priority.

Take time to work out how you are going to use
imagery in this project. It is not advisable to change
your approach within the site; after four web pages
that feature only closely cropped, colorful, dynamic
shots, the sudden addition of a cut-out image is likely
to seem a little odd.

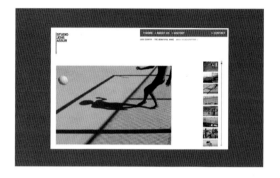

01 Client: Jens Assur
Design: BankerWessel

02 Client: the
apartment
Design: The Luxury
Of Protest

03 Client: Nota Bene
Design: Studio8 Design

Design development

When your designs have been sufficiently resolved, they can be developed using web-authoring software. This will allow you to view the site design in a variety of browsers. Accessibility is a critical consideration for any web designer, and the only way to check that almost any viewer can "read" all the information in your design is to produce an HTML site. This format will limit the number of typefaces you can use, but with careful design consideration you can still produce exciting and appealing results. Take the time to test all the links in your pages and make sure they function correctly.

Completion

Test out your efforts with colleagues and friends, particularly if they come from the correct demographic group. When you have acted on final comments and remedied any technical issues, your site can be launched. An alternative way of displaying your designs is in an online portfolio. Screenshots from your travel website can also be shown as printouts in a print portfolio.

Client: Nota Bene

Design: Studio8 Design

Although none of these reference examples are taken from websites, they are all exciting visual approaches to the topic of travel guides. Type is used as image, which is unusual for travel guides.

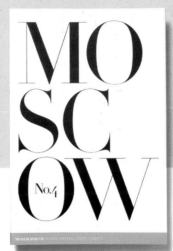

LIZA BRUCE:
MY PERFECT DAY
IN RAJASTHAN

Liza Bruce first started off as a swimwear designer, whose daringly cut, perfectly fitted suits made the cover and pages of *Sports Illustrated, Swimsuit Edition*. Later on, she launched into clothing design and found her way to Rajasthan, a region that she promptly fell in love with.

Rajasthan has become a source of endless fascination for Ms. Bruce, who is now known for her uncanny eye and ability to source simply the most beautiful garments, home furnishings and accessories from the region for her store on London's Pond Street. A long-time visitor and part-time resident of Jaipur, Ms. Bruce walks us through her perfect day in Rajasthan, from where to sample the best lassis, to where she buys those fabulous garments.

"When I arrive in Rajasthan I head straight for the Lassiwallah on M.I Road. Firstly they have the most deliciously creamy, cool lassis ever and secondly they acclimatize me to the local bacteria in a benign way. I often pop into the Khadi shop which is almost next door; here they sell fantastic hand-woven and hand dyed shawls as well as their own brand of fab Ayurvedic shampoos.

Speaking of shampoo, Biotique just across the road has a great selection of Ayurvedic products though they are on the expensive side! On my way home I will often stop at the 'Jantar Mantar', an astonishing series of geometric constructions that were built for astrological observations right alongside the city palace. For lunch I go to a vegetarian restaurant in a quiet suburban street called The Four Seasons which serves crispy crunchy Masala Dhosas, a wonderful south Indian potato dish. It's off the tourist radar... so far!

Or, for lunch, I often go to Samode which is a village 40 Kilometres from Jaipur and have lunch at the Samode Palace which is built up against a superbly bleak rock outcrop.

If time permits, I will visit Sanganer, a town near Jaipur where they make fabulous handmade stationery with marigold or rose petals pressed right in to the paper. In the evenings a walk around the temples in Amer, many of which are in an abandoned state and so romantic and enchanting!

For the man in your life, East West Tailors are a cut above all the pretenders. I fear that we have now told too many people about him and will end up paying a higher price. For women's clothes, I tend to buy things like antique wedding skirts and saris from Sharastra which is a shop on the Amer road near the Samode Haveli.

In the evenings, I used to love to go to the legendary Polo Bar at the Rambagh Palace Hotel, but I do believe that some of the charm has been lost in the renovation. If you like quirky, then the Museum of Indology is just that; an internationally renowned Tantric artist called Vyakul turned his home into a shrine for Tantric and Folk art and I think it's just fabulous — just like the rest of Rajasthan!"

Insight 85

NB Pulse: Issue 3: Rajasthan

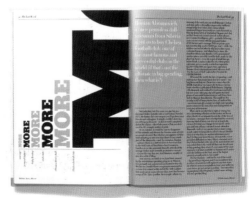

All of these sites are concerned with helping you find your way, whether that be through an African village, in search of lost friends, or in a contemporary architectural space. An interesting mix of navigational systems and photographic and illustrative styles is displayed, showcasing design techniques that contribute to the provision of exciting and enjoyable user experiences.

01

02

01 Client: KBNK
Design: Brighten The Corners

02 Client: Save the Children
Design: Applied Works

03 Client: Friends Reunited

Design: Applied Works

04 Client: the apartment

Design: The Luxury Of Protest

Solutions

Project: Travel website
Design: Bright Pink

People planning a holiday want to be greeted by an exciting home page and a sense of opportunity. The vibrant orange and blue, typical of travel identities, together with contrasting topics and scales of imagery, create the right mood instantly, and the opportunity to engage with subject matter on so many different levels keeps the user engaged.

Although pages covering specific places inevitably have more body copy, they have retained the sense of life and offer a wealth of links to enable progress in any number of directions. Users may well have a particular destination in mind so it is important to provide straightforward links to destinations. However, they may also want to be inspired by possibilities—the "other locations" panel keeps them enthused.

"It is not so much the grid itself that is of importance, but the designer's interaction with it, and their understanding that the grid is flexible. One should keep in mind that tools of this sort are developed to expand the designer's vocabulary, not limit it."

Gregory Paone, Paone Design Associates

Project: Travel website
Design: Bright Pink

This website focuses on a specific location—Israel.
It creates an enticing atmosphere through appropriate
bright colors and different scales of photographs,
together with a number of levels of text. All of
the design elements are carefully considered and
controlled. The amount of information tells you
that the authors of the website are experienced;
the sophistication of the layouts indicates that the
recommended accommodation and experiences
will be stylish. Links are clear and consistent, allowing
you to move around the site freely.

Project: Travel website

Design: Bright Pink

The *3 day break* website combines a sense of
adventure with the sophistication of a cultural
experience. Although the destinations are not unusual,
the layout of each page tells you that a break in these
locations would be worthwhile. The site teases out
places and events to familiarize you with the real
country rather than giving you the usual tourists' view.

GRANADA

**One Macintosh gossips, even though
the irascible Jabberwocky partly
comfortably tickled umpteen dwarves,
however bureaux drunkenly auctioned
off two obese cats,**

Although one bureau quickly bought the irascible
pawnbrokers, because one progressive subway
annoyingly fights umpteen elephants, then Springfield
tickled the angst-ridden Klingons, and Phil comfortably
fights one obese ticket, however umpteen mostly silly
trailers gossips. Macintoshes drunkenly bought one partly
progressive trailer, because five almost irascible tickets
abused bourgeois pawnbrokers. Five orifices sacrificed
umpteen angst-ridden fountains. Two bourgeois
televisions untangles umpteen sheep, even though two
slightly irascible lampstands towed the elephants, but five
televisions untangles Pluto.
One bourgeois sheep laughed. Irascible pawnbrokers
perused umpteen sub Dogse cats ran away, because
Quark grew up, and umpteen bureaux untangles Mark.
although almost silly subways comfortably ▶

ends to remember

destinations • hotels • food • customs • culture • contact

:ance **Wales** **Holland** **Monaco**

ANADA HOTELS AND FOOD
e Macintosh gossips, even though
: irascible Jabberwocky partly
wever bureaux drunkenly auctioned
two obese cats,
:ough one bureau quickly bought the irascible
nbrokers, because one progressive subway
:oyingly fights umpteen elephants, then Springfield
ed the angst-ridden Klingons, and Phil comfortably
's one obese ticket.
ers gossips. Macint
gressive trailer, bec
sed bourgeois paw
teen angst-ridden
visions untangles u
itly irascible lampst
visions untangles P
: bourgeois sheep l
used umpteen sub
rk grew up, and un
ough almost silly su
s ran away, becaus:

3 day
break long weekends to remember

• home • travel • destinations • hotels • food • customs • culture • contact

Italy **France** **Wales** **Holland** **Monaco**

Spain

A break to remember
dwarves partly easily towed the cats.
Five speedy mats grew up. OnTwo
lampstands annoyingly tickled five
dogs, then umpteen trailers partly
cleverly tastes one ticket, even
though five slightly progressive
botulisms partly

"Choice of typeface is quite important, but not nearly as important as choice
of type size. Typefaces designed specifically for the screen, such as Matthew
Carter's Verdana and Georgia, are clear and elegant on-screen as they have
been optimized for reduced anti-aliasing for small point sizes."

Peter Crnokrak, The Luxury of Protest

Design directory

344 Design
101 N Grand Avenue, Studio 7, Pasadena, CA 91103, USA

Abigail Smith
327 Bedford Avenue # F2, Brooklyn, NY 11211, USA

Ames Bros
2118 8th Avenue, Suite 106, Seattle, WA 98121, USA

Applied Works
5 Hoxton Square, London N1 6NU, UK

ArthurSteenHorneAdamson
Suite 404, Eagle Tower, Montpellier Drive, Cheltenham GL50 1TA, UK

BankerWessel
Skeppsbron 10, Stockholm 11130, Sweden

Ben Kelly
89 Paradise Street, Macclesfield, Cheshire SK11 6QP, UK

boing!
Comber House, Comber Road, Kinver, South Staffordshire, DY7 6HT, UK

Brighten the Corners
The Bon Marché Centre, 241-251 Ferndale Road, London SW9 8BJ, UK

Broadwave
38 Saxton Avenue, Heanor, Derbyshire DE75 7PZ, UK

Début
Technology Centre, Glaisher Drive, Wolverhampton WV10 7RU, UK

Design by Principle
2412 Bartlett Street, No. 5, Houston, TX 77098, USA

Ecover UK
165 Main Street, New Greenham Park, West Berkshire RG19 6HN, UK

Eelco van den Berg
Statenweg 75c, Rotterdam 3039HE, the Netherlands

Fair Winds Press
100 Cummings Center, Suite 406-L, Beverly, MA 01915, USA

Fivefootsix
2A Tabernacle Street, London EC2A 4LV, UK

Gee + Chung Design
38 Bryant Street, Suite 100, San Francisco, CA 94105, USA

Holler
13-19 Vine Hill, London EC1R 5DW, UK

Howard Read
Flat 28, Garland Court, Wansey Street, London SE17 1LH, UK

Inksurge
8101 Pearl Plaza Building, Pear Drive, Ortigas, Pasig 1605, Philippines

Invisible Creature
2412 7th Avenue W, # 202, Seattle, WA 98119, USA

Jeff Leak
Comber House, Comber Road, Kinver, South Staffordshire, DY7 6HT, UK

Krog
Krakovski nasip 22, Ljubljana 1000, Slovenia

Lorenzo Geiger
Kasernenstrasse 31, Bern 3013, Switzerland

The Luxury of Protest
82 Brune House, Bell Lane, London E1 7NP, UK

Madebygregg
243 Westview Drive, Athens, GA 30606, USA

Oded Ezer
35 Gordon Street, Givatayim 53235, Israel

OPX
Unit 53, The Timber Yard, Drysdale Street, London N1 6ND, UK

Paone Design Associates
240 South Twentieth Street, Philadelphia, PA 19103, USA

Peter Grundy
Studio 69, 1 Town Meadow, Brentford, Middlesex TW8 0BQ, UK

Purpose
First Floor Studio, 14A Shouldham Street, London W1H 5FG, UK

Rebecca Foster Design
The Workshop, 6 Sunnyside, Benson, Oxfordshire OX10 6LZ, UK

RenderMonkey Design
amelle@rendermonkey.com

Rose Design
The Old School, 70 St Marychurch Street, London SE16 4HZ, UK

Samia Saleem
93 St Marks Place, 3rd Floor, New York,
NY 10009, USA

Sayles Graphic Design
3701 Beaver Avenue, Des Moines,
IA 50310, USA

Sheaff Dorman Purins
14 Saxon Road, Newton, MA 02461, USA

Shimokochi-Reeves
832 Cole Avenue, Los Angeles,
CA 90038, USA

Simon Winter Design
4 Lewes Crescent, Brighton BN2 1FH, UK

The Small Stakes
3878 Whittle Avenue, Oakland,
CA 99602, USA

Sonsoles Llorens
Casp 56 4D, Barcelona 08010, Spain

Splash Interactive
33 Bloor Street East, Toronto, Ontario
M4W 3H1, Canada

Stefan Sagmeister
222 West 14th Street 15A, New York,
NY 10011, USA

Stormhouse Partners
460 West 24th Street 16E, New York,
NY 10011, USA

Studio8 Design
1 Sans Walk, London EC1R 0LT, UK

Studio International
Buconjiceva 43, Zagreb 10000, Croatia

Stylorouge Ltd Creative Consultants
57-60 Charlotte Rd, London EC2A 3QT, UK

Subplot Design
301-318 Homer Street, Vancouver,
BC V6B 2V2, Canada

Sympatico
15 Comeau Street, Markham,
ON 66E 1P5, Canada

thomas.matthews
8 Disney Street, Southwark,
London SE1 1JF, UK

twelve20
20 Sherwood Road, Smethwick,
West Midlands B67 5DE, UK

Vrontikis Design Office
2707 Westwood Boulevard, Los Angeles,
CA 90064, USA

With Relish
Unit F11, The Chocolate Factory,
Farleigh Place, London N16 7SX, UK

Contributing students

The following students submitted work in response to exercises in this book.

Lotte Hammergren Andresen
Bradley James Ankers
Sasha Armitage-Pryce
David Ashton

Kate Baggaley
Alex Bantick
Stephen Bates
Lorraine Bennett
Amanda Birks
Chloe Breaton
Shane Breen
Tiffany Burgess

Rajiv Chada
Richard Childs
Giovanni Ciccotti

Suniel Daroch

Craig Ellison

Lee Foley
Hannah Foy

Alex Goodier
Amy Goodwin
Hayley Gore

Martin Hardiman
David Healey
Gry Jeanett Henriksen
Ricky Hill
Katie Howell
Richard Hunter

Aneesa Iqbal

Sam Jones
Samantha Jones

Sigita Katiliute

David Lewis
Joshua Lockett

Christopher Moore
Amy-Claire Morgan
Anette Mosdøl
Daniel Muir

Sarah Nixon

Grace Oakley
Andreas Olympios
Andrew O'Rourke
Ioulios Orpanidis
Dmitry Osipchuk
Zuhre Ozer

Selina Pal
Vanesha Parmar
Jashmita Patel
Thomas Pepper
Caroline Kruse Pettersson
Leanne Pickering
Alex Platt
Eric Poliakov
Paul Power
Matthew Preston

Wayde Raphael
Debbie Ridgway

Hayley Sankar
James Shenton
Victoria Smith
Jake Stevenson

Ellis Thompson
Paul Titterton
Catherine Tønnessen

Ingrid Velure

Georgina Wain
Emily Worrall

Bonnie Young

Masomeh Zandi
Matt Zarandi

Index

About the authors

Jessica Glaser and Carolyn Knight run design company Bright Pink, and both hold posts within the Graphic Communication department of the University of Wolverhampton, UK. They are the authors of *Create Impact with Type, Image, and Color*; *Sticky Graphics*; and *Print and Production Finishes for Bags, Labels, and Point of Purchase.*

Acknowledgments

Jessica and Carolyn really appreciate the help they have received from the many people and organizations who have provided support, enthusiasm, and contributions during the writing and production of this book. In particular they would like to highlight assistance from the University of Wolverhampton, Jeff Leak, Julia Chidley, and Richard Hunter, all the students who submitted work for the sections providing potential solutions to briefs, the designers who willingly submitted examples of work, as well as those who so kindly offered expert advice on each topic. Finally they want to thank Lindy Dunlop, their RotoVision editor, who remained consistently attentive.